To Gary Voet

Best Wishes,

Larry Stanton

Glory Days of
BAJA

Glory Days of

BAJA

Coyotes, Cactus, Mosquitoes & Mud

Larry Stanton

DESIGNED BY WENDY L. TRUBIA

ISBN 1-887269-05-3

LIBRARY OF CONGRESS CATALOG
CARD NUMBER: 95-83173

JOHN CULLER & SONS
P.O. BOX 1277
CAMDEN, SOUTH CAROLINA 29020
1-800-861-9188

Dedication

To Paul, who left us early, but was the first to deke out the big pond in the sky.

Prologue

Poco a poco, or "little by little," as it translates, refers to "easy does it," or the laid back quality of Mexican life. If something doesn't get done today, there is always *mānana*. Compare that to the hustle and bustle of American life, and the difference is a much greater intake of antihypertensives and Rolaids north of the border.

The following is a chronicle of hunting and fishing stories that took place in Baja over the past quarter century. At age 50 it seems incredible that I have already been able to enjoy the magnificent peninsula for half of my life. Events in the following chapters are but a tiny fragment of the hundreds of stories that have taken place as a result of multiple *entradas* into Baja.

To help in character identification – and believe me there are some real characters – a list of friends and hunters includes Curran, Brown, Braith, Dan, Palmer, Barr, Stewart, and Lee. Lupe, the central Mexican character, was probably fifteen or so when we first met in 1969, so he is near forty today. His immediate family includes his father, Don Emilio; Mamacita (or Refugio), his mom; and El Señor, his grandfather; who has lived with the family the entire 25 years I have known them.

As they say, several of the names have been changed to protect the *guilty*.

Contents

Cascabel

urran, you look like hell. Are you sure you want to go? You know it's not like we didn't just get back last weekend, and we're headed down again next week."

"Stanton, you wanna drive or talk? Now drive, dammit, and wake me when it's time to hunt."

The trip down from San Diego was uneventful but inspiring; the magnificent mile high bouldered hills through which Highway Eight passed, sloped gently to the south, right into Baja. We continued through Devil's Canyon, a cooker anytime, but this late August day sent the thermometer well past 115 degrees. As we descended down into the lush Imperial Valley, the vistas became increasingly more majestic. The Salton Sea, becoming more saline by the year, now glimmered as a jewel in the afternoon sun. Hundreds of square miles of forest green row crops stood out against the stark adjacent desert. And always, just off to the south, lay Baja. A couple of times I checked Curran's forehead, and it was apparent he had at least a 102 degree fever. But like he said, if he had to die, make it in Baja, prop him up against a tree, and put a shotgun in his hands.

We crossed the border uneventfully, no mean feat; headed south through the slumbering giant, Mexicali, then headed east once the Chocolate Mountains came down to the asphalt to meet us. In the heat of day the Chocolates are dumpy brown and unmercifully hot. But as evening comes, they take on a spectacular purple-brown hue, which is best left seen than described. Another hour east, through Durango, then to the Carranza stoplight, and we again headed south.

Carranza, what a place. The stoplight looked like early 1930's and was without paint, 30 degrees off the vertical, and most significantly, was without electricity. Not that there was *electricidad* anywhere else in town, but the stoplight was special. Imagine for a moment, a four way stop in the middle of Jesus only knows where, pancake flat desert for miles, six twig shacks (one with corrugated tin roof), and this ridiculous, magnificent stoplight. In later years there would be paint at the concrete base, but only when some local citizen with a few Tecates on board parked his car around the base of the light at 30 miles an hour. As long as I can remember, though, that light has always been there. It was a greeter of sorts, because from here south, we were only 45 minutes to hunting.

Remembering the first time through Carranza one cold late wintry afternoon in 1969, Braith and I actually saw the birth of the village. It was a puzzlement of uncommon proportions. Headed south out of town and pulled over into the desert were six large flatbed trucks, complete with greatly oversized wood slats to allow for triple and quadruple the average safe load. Typically these same trucks would carry cotton, bulging to twice the width of the truck's bed and stacked two to three times the height of the cab, making them exceedingly unstable. But this time they carried *campesinos*, dark skinned men from the interior, mostly Indians, and all entrusted with some crude tool. We arrived basically within minutes of them, and watched in wonderment as they dug a sleeping space, down below the bone-chilling wind, and later as it turned out, close to the warmth of the campfire. There were no suitcases, no handbags, *puro nada*. The desert floor gets cold at night, and these folks had tattered cottons on, none of which were longsleeved. We passed on, shot several pheasants for camp meat, made camp, and wondered that night beneath a billion stars exactly what the hey was going on back there. The weekend hunt, sandwiched in between internship's 36 hours on/ 36 hours off routine was relaxing, exhilarating and rejuvenating. After the hunt we headed slowly back through Carranza, and were amazed at the industry of these new arrivals. In one and a half days they had constructed eight twig and mud huts, all with central campfires, and had begun hoeing weeds and *chamiso* with a resultant dozen hand made rows several hundred feet long, artfully fashioned, and ready for planting. These guys had been there barely a day and a half, built their shelters, and already had some part of a field ready for sowing. There were no women then, nor children. Just some hard working peasants looking for a better life. My God, from what meagerness did they come?

As we drove by, their faces showed neither friendship, enmity, nor even curiosity. We saw determination and we saw nothing. With succeeding trips, we saw weekly improvements – a communal latrine, corrugated tin to replace the twigs, thatched roofs, and much, much later, cement with windows, and other modern conveniences. I often wondered if those same bold men who spent that first wintry night under the stars, were the same ones to finally move into a cement 15 foot x 15 foot block house, complete with windows. I hoped so...

. Once past Carranza the road curved past the long deserted army barracks in the distance, and cut straight through the Colorado River. Naturally, this was not the main branch of the Colorado, but it was always impressive, especially in a VW bug. This trip, however, we were in the green *Chile Relleño*, a minimally green, mostly rusted, old International four wheel drive, with pop up camper shell behind. We bumped along the concrete roadway bottom, had the engine cough a few times to protest this vehicular maltreatment, and fifteen minutes later we were in Sombrerete. Although fluent in Spanish, I have always wondered if it weren't meant to be "Sombrerito" or "little hat." But the three families there claimed no, it was just plain Sombrerete, and didn't mean anything. And when I thought about it, most of the towns I've lived in never meant anything either. Still I think of Sombrerete, a sonorous name, as sleepy little hat.

We were now three and a half hours into the trip and Curran had taken the shakes, so I had him swill some Gatorade, aspirin and penicillin, then headed south on Schoolhouse Road (years later we finally located an abandoned schoolhouse). Well, maybe not road exactly, but at least it was well travelled and you could easily follow the dirt tracks. Three canals later, we headed west, right into the Chocolates, by now becoming a bluish purple. There had been a cornfield we'd spotted the previous week, but had been unable to hunt due to the late hour.

As we inched forward, I would turn the engine off to listen for the heart pounding ERRK! ERRRRK! of the cock pheasant. This was no longer a road but just desert and *chamiso* and whoops! The right front tire was in the slop in the middle of the desert, adjacent to the greenest cornfield you ever would want to see. I shut down, checked Curran, (he was still breathing), and went hunting.

Even though we had been going less than the speedometer could read we had become mired in mud from irrigation water that had flooded a whole lot more than just corn. Curran said go on, so I set out, first inspecting for sign (white splashed droppings or the telltale three toed pheasant track) and ERRRRRK! God, that was close, but nothing flew, and in the desert, sound can be tricky. Sometimes it can be like eight track stereo, and sometimes it is nothing. I walked slowly toward the edge of the corn, and I heard him break through the green stalks. Faster now, I ran ahead through the water, peering as far as the *chamiso* would let me see with intermittent clumps of brush and weeds. Well, I know for a fact that pheasants don't like to be in water, so this beauty was holed up in one of these *chamiso* clumps, and I had suddenly cut his tracks. By now it was mid-afternoon, somewhere in the 110 to 120 degree category and that pheasant had gone to cover. Well, we'll see about that. The clump ahead was surrounded by more dry desert than any other and instinctively, I planned the stalk. Cover to my left – he would fly that way if spooked, but most likely he would get in the middle of that *chamiso* and just sit tight.

I came in from the left with a perfect 270 degree field of fire, ready for when he jumped up. Jeez, the only other thing he could do is swim. The splashing water was giving my location away though, putting us on a more equal footing. The best bet was to proceed slowly, then jump on the dry area behind the *chamiso* clump, and be ready for whatever. Whew! Whatever! As I jumped to the dry earth I had the startling realization that I was sharing six feet of dry desert with a six foot rattlesnake. And he was not amused; he was not about to get wet, was pissed off that I had ended his peaceful sun bath – all nice and stretched out as he was. I took very uncareful aim and shot his head off. With a shotgun it's not all that hard. The head was gone, but the body went nuts. Writhing, coiling, rattling, striking – just minus his head. I watched mesmerized for what seemed like forever, but was probably just a few minutes. I picked him up, still coiling, writhing, and headed back to the truck with dinner. When I got there Curran was still lying on the front seat out cold, and didn't respond when I called, so I threw the rattler on him. The snake went crazy; Curran jumped straight up, smashed into the mirror and dashboard, screaming "Arrgh! Aarrrgh! Aarrghhhhhh!" Finally he saw me and assessed the situation; his head now cleared, he looked me right in the eyes, and... smiled.

We stood there for a moment like that, this whimsical little smile playing at the corners of his mouth, and then he skinned the rattler and said, "Let's eat." To this day I marvel at what superhuman control it must have taken to not jump out of the truck and throttle my miserable ass. But Curran was tough; Navy Seal tough, to be exact, one of those rare guys who went to Nam looking for a fight, found it, then kicked butt. A man's man, the kind of guy you'd want in the foxhole next to yours. Tough. Mean. Courageous. Deadly. And, he had a long memory...

As his radiology residency years rolled by, we hunted dozens more times throughout Baja, but usually we'd return somewhere near the swamps, to camp, hunt, tell lies, and enjoy a camaraderie that only the campfire could bring. And then, one June, it was over. With his residency now completed, Curran accepted a job up in Porterville (where?), almost twelve hours from the Mexican border. He still would come down occasionally, but I didn't hear from him much after that . Then, one crisp spring morning some three or four years later, the phone rang. It was Curran.

"Hey, Stanton. Get up here Friday morning and we're going to fly in by chopper to the middle fork of the Kings River. Virgin trout, inaccessible except by eight day's hike, and a veteran helicopter pilot from Nam. Bring warm gear, we'll be sleeping next to the river." And he hung up.

Thursday night late I managed to find Porterville, and met the rest of the crew – Asher, also a radiologist, who had been a carrier based fighter pilot in Viet Nam; Maureen, Curran's girlfriend; and Ron, the pilot; plus two others. The plan was to drive to the foothills of the Sierras early Friday, then Ron would ferry us into the middle fork of the Kings country. To save on trips, Ron and one person were inside the chopper, and gear and one person each side were lashed on outside. Curran rode in the chopper; you know where my spot was. Lifting off was hairy, but once in the air it was magnificent. One range after another flashed by, and in a heartbeat we were there. The descent, however, was another matter. As the sun came up, convection and conduction currents were beginning to whip up the winds out of the canyon, first up, then down, then right, then left. It was the original "E" ticket ride at Disneyland. Then, just at the appropriate moment, down we went like a quarter in a telephone slot, except with less room to spare. Lashed to the chopper's undercarriage, I watched those mountainsides slide by as we dropped into the canyon. Obviously Ron was one helluva pilot. But later that night between drinks, when asked if he'd ever done this before, he shook his head and said "nope."

We set up camp, fished, cooked, drank, sat around the campfire, told lies, drank some more, and literally passed out. I don't remember being put on my cot, undressed and put in my sleeping bag, yet that's where I was when Curran woke me the next morning at first light and said "let's go fishing." I sat up, undid the bottom zipper of my 10 degree down bag to let some air in, looked at Curran and said, "Later." Sometime after I was dreaming, back in Baja; the sun now well above the canyon rim had started to warm the river bed floor and us. It was heavenly. It was otherworldly; nothing could be this serene, this relaxing, this...Oh God, what was that? No, it was nothing; It moved again, next to my leg; hell, that's around my leg! Oh, sweet Jesus, there's something in my bag. I can't be this hungover and AAAAAhh! AAAAhhh! AAhhh! There's a snake in my mummy bag and he's coiling up my waist. AAAAhhh!AAAAhh! AAAAhh! I fumbled for the zipper – these bags are warm, but they are not built for rapid exit. I found it, unzipped the top and squirted out of the bag with snake attached. Help! Help! Help me! I rolled over and over on the river bed, and finally got this miserable reptile off me, to the shouts, hoots, and laughter of my travelling companions. Dazed, I collected my thoughts, balled up my fists, and was about to behead the closest reveller, when I spotted Curran. There was that little smile playing again at the corners of his mouth. He just sat there and smiled, didn't say anything, but I knew. All these years later, we were even.

El General

Timmy had been bugging me two months now. "Geez, Larry, when you gonna take me to Baja, huh, huh, huh?" He and his family lived three doors down but he always found reasons to hang around our garage, especially by my hunting gear. At 16, he was a good kid, and did okay in school. He was no Einstein, but had that personal magnetism – charm, some people call it – that made you look forward to his visits. Polite, always eager to help, and fascinated by the treks into Baja, he just had to see it for himself.

So just before Christmas, I told him we were a go for a four day trip. The only catch was we'd be coming home the night of the 24th – Christmas Eve – late. He said, "No sweat," and his mother packed him off with candy bars, cookies, and sardines. Six hours later we were making camp. Not only was this Timmy's first hunt, but it was also his first time away from home. I was to find this out later – in spades. By four that morning we were in the pond, pulling our duck boat through two inches of water and twelve inches of mud toward the "flats;" no motor could be run here. Sprig, or pintail, as they are called, will work the advancing waterline, and two to three inches of water is just ideal for them. I had found a small lagoon at the southeast end of Duarte pond the previous week, noted the sprig flight path went over it, and planned deking it out the next time down. When we were within a couple hundred yards, my heart jumped as I saw several hundred duck bodies already there. The moonlight shimmered off their... feathers? No way. Feathers don't reflect light like that. Hell, those were decoys. Someone else's.

So we backtracked about a quarter of a mile, found some brush, and deked out. Toward the end of December, first light doesn't come until late. On cue, at 5:45, first light, the very best time to have birds decoy in, four hunters came splashing through our dekes and headed for their blind to the south. Obviously they had been there the previous day, and left their decoys out.

Timmy got a real show; flight after flight of gadwall, pintail, teal, widgeon – even a couple of redheads – looked us over; but due to the guys still splashing through the mud, they just dipped their wings and were gone. The boys south of us had an interesting setup, by the way. Around this little cove in the tules they had chosen to make four blinds, each man shooting alone instead of the usual two. The advantage of two men per blind is simply that the entire horizon can be watched if you stand back to back. But, what the heck, these guys were probably retired because they had come down on Wednesday, a day earlier than we could manage, so more power to them.

We watched a glorious sunrise – one of my very favorite parts of duck hunting in Baja – and we also watched their decoy spread suck those ducks in like iron filings to a magnet. I was right about their spot; it was right smack dab in the middle of the flyway. Timmy nailed a seagull, which I threatened to make him eat. Like he said, "Looked like a duck to me."

The tip of the sun burst forth, seemingly coming up right out of the swamp. It was indescribably powerful, peaceful, serene. Just the occasional *"boom, boom"* to the south of us interrupted the solitude. It had been cold, but with the sunrise and warmth, and still feeling the effects of last night's six hour drive and no sleep – Timmy had asked questions all night – I started to nod off. My chin was on my chest when my reverie was rudely interrupted by a high pitched whine and deafening roar, coming fast out of the northwest. Airboat! (In later years Mikey and I had one also, but hunting just wasn't the same). Two hour mud slogs in the dark, pulling your boat – now that's hunting. Anyway, we watched this guy approach from two miles away, hell bent for leather, making a beeline for the boys just south of us. Every duck in Baja lifted off the pond and headed elsewhere as the airboat neared. I thought he was going to rip right through these guys' blinds, but he stopped some twenty yards short of them, killed the motor, and casually began throwing out dekes. From the blind farthest from him, the hunter stepped out and said, "Hey, asshole, what the hell do you think you're doing?"

"Hey, screw you, Jack. I hunted here last week!"

"Yeah, well you sure as hell aren't hunting here this week."

"Oh no? Well just hide and watch. I hunt wherever I damn well please. Fuck you."

"You put another decoy out and I'm gonna shoot it."

At which point the airboat wizard bends over, comes up with his shotgun, jacks two shells in, and lets fly in the general direction of the far blind. Virtually in unison the other three hunters rose up and pelted that idiot in the airboat with everything they had. He hit the deck and they must have hit his airboat with at least a hundred shells. On about the fourth or fifth reload, the airboat guy kneeled up and started pulling frantically on the engine starter rope. The airplane motor fired, coughed, and then died. The boys in the blinds peppered him again a few more times for good measure, then all stood up and had a real gut laugh. The airboat driver managed to propel his boat a few feet with each cough of the engine, but try as he might, he could not get that motor to function. When we last saw him, he was still pulling on the darned starter rope, advancing northward five feet per pull. Timmy's eyes were big as saucers. "Wow! It's really dangerous hunting, huh?" On the trip back in, I was not looking forward to stewed seagull for lunch, so when four teal whistled overhead, two well placed long leads brought all four down. "Nice shootin', Tim."

"But I don't think I shot."

"Yeah, you did. Anyway, they'll all taste the same over the campfire."

We hit camp around noon, famished. Timmy had already had six candy bars, two cokes, and two bags of cookies for breakfast, and the long walk in had gotten his appetite going. Timmy offered how he didn't know if he could eat duck; they smelled kinda funny. Kinda like, you know, poop. I assured him that was from being gut shot, and a little cleaning would take care of it. He didn't know, and was hungry besides, so as I cooked, he opened up a can of cold cream of mushroom soup and ate the congealed globs along with another Butterfingers bar. Whew! This kid was tough.

There are probably hundreds of duck recipes, most of them very ordinary to not-so-good, but there are a couple dozen that are truly world beaters. One of my favorites, Teal Picheguila, is from the Mexican mainland and it's a dilly. The four teal breasts were being grilled over the oak fire with a marinade of lemon butter and garlic salt. The trick, as in cooking most game, is not to overcook it. I didn't, and after a peanut butter and jelly sandwich, glass of milk, and tin of sardines, Timmy tried one and admitted that it wasn't all that bad. Then he had another candy bar, two cokes, a bag of peanuts, and said,"You know, it didn't taste bad, but it kind of upset my stomach."

The next two days were spent hunting upland game: quail, pheasant, and doves, or as Timmy said, "whatever flew." Timmy was progressing poorly with the gamebird identification lessons. By late afternoon of the third day, he reminded me of a veteran birder filling out his bird identification list, except with dead specimens. Starling, blackbird, magpie, meadowlark – "Jesus, Timmy, that's a songbird" – plus several species of that delicacy, sparrow; this was to go along with his now decaying seagull.

"Timmy. Gamebirds, son, gamebirds."

The thrill of the hunt, the campfire, eating candy bars all day long – it was magical for Timmy. When the sun finally went down on Christmas eve we reluctantly headed the old Dodge van for home. Tired but eager to get home for Christmas, a glitch appeared as we entered Mexicali. It seemed we weren't the only ones planning to cross the border that night. The cars and trucks, usually backed up for several miles from the border crossing, met us as we came to the southern city limits.

"Holy smokers, Timmy. I've seen some lines, but never anything like this." By my guess we were at least twelve miles from the border crossing. The geniuses at the border had picked tonight to close ten of the twelve auto exits.

"It's Christmas." Wow. After an hour we had moved maybe a couple of hundred yards closer, when I spotted the cutoff sign to Tijuana. Highway Two went through the mountains and la Rumorosa, then to the unhurried crossing at the quaint little village of Tecate, a hundred miles west of us. At the first break in traffic, I did a U-turn and we headed west. The partially lit overhead sign read "Tijuana 200 Km." It was the last bit of light we were to see for some time.

Now one of the reasons for hunting with two or more is so that on the return trip, the other guy can help keep the driver awake. Three miles out of town, I called, "Timmy. Are you awake son? Timmy?" No Timmy. He was completely gone, asleep and unarousable. With the mountain switchbacks, the unmarked center line, the narrowing of the road to one lane in spots, no radio ('62 Dodge van, remember), the driving went from tough to ugly. Then exactly at 4,000 feet elevation, it started to snow through an impenetrable fog. Yikes, maybe this was why everybody was crossing in Mexicali. We crept forward for what seemed two lifetimes. No worry about falling asleep now; it was too damn cold. Cold enough that Timmy came up front and said,"Hey, turn on the heat."

"Be my guest."

"No heater, huh?"

"Nope."

"Look, Tim, just help keep an eye out. I darn near can't see the road most of the time. Snow's got everything all messed up."

With no heater, we also had no defroster and the snow started to pile up on the windshield. And then in a flash, he was there. This fat Mexican army guy in baggy pants and shirt, was waving his outstretched arms at us to stop. I jammed on the brakes and we skidded slowly towards him. He looked, then waved us through, and I noticed the sign, la Rumorosa. I stepped on the accelerator, slowly, when "*Whirr, whirr, whirr, whump, whump, whump!*" A siren went off, lights came on everywhere, and we were instantly surrounded by two dozen Mexican army regulars, all advancing on us with submachine guns. Man! I hit the brakes, turned off the ignition, and raised my hands to the ceiling. Timmy was so stunned that he just sat there and stared; seeing, but not registering.

A well dressed soldier of some importance approached us with his pistol drawn. "*Afuera!*" We got out and stood there with our hands raised as the soldiers surrounded, then frisked us.

"*A donde van?*"

"We are going to Huntington Beach. We live there."

"*Por la Rumorosa?*"

"Yes, well the border at Mexicali was about a six hour wait, so I thought this would be quicker."

"What were you doing in Baja?"

"Hunting."

"You have guns?"

"*Sí.*"

To the other soldiers he said, "*Adentro,*" and they

25

opened the van and unloaded everything into the mud and slush. My beautiful fleece-lined gun case lay in the mud and water, but I bit my tongue. This was not the time.

"*Capitan*. What are you looking for? Why are you holding us?"

"I am not the *capitan*.. He is inside."

At which point, arms still raised, we marched inside. It was cold out there, especially with light weight hunting clothing on, and Timmy's teeth began to chatter. And not just from the cold, I suspected. When we entered the building, Timmy was separated from me and placed in a jail cell just behind the *comandante*. One look and I knew he had had it. The boy was scared and was trembling. Just a minute and the tears would come. The first sobs came as the *comandante* spoke. "You have drugs? How long have you been carrying drugs? Where did you buy them? Who sold them to you ?"

"*Capitan*, we have been hunting. We have Mexican hunting licenses, we have registered Mexican gun permits, and we have game birds to declare."

Now la Rumorosa is nothing more than a wide spot in the road. There is no entertainment there, no eateries, no nothing. It is a military checkpoint. In the cold, in the snow, with two dozen other Mexican soldiers on Christmas eve, it is a punishment, or worse, a humiliation, to serve there. As the night wore on I kinda figured the *capitan* was pissed that he had drawn this very inglorious duty tour in this ... this no place.

A sergeant brought in our papers, permits, licenses, gun, ammo, and birds. Now, whereas I had prevailed upon Timmy to leave the seagulls and meadowlarks behind, we did have a full complement of birds: 30 doves, 30 ducks, and 15 quail, exactly the number permitted by my license. However, when it came to ammo count, it appeared we had three more shells than the two hundred allowable, plus we had seventy-five dead birds to boot.

"*Una problema, senor*. How did you kill all these birds

and still have three cartridges too many as permitted by your license?"

God, I was tempted to say that we had fed them poison corn, but this wasn't the time for wisecracks.

"Hmm. Maybe we're bringing some shells home that we left here last trip down."

Timmy had stopped crying now. He was staring down at the floor, looking at the bars in the cell, and shaking his head. He had followed our conversation, but realized we had a problem with the shell count. "Yeah, that's right, Larry. I remember loading those shells up that you had buried down there."

"*Cállete*! When I want this boy to speak I will ask him. You, my friend, are going to jail. You are going to stay here a long time. We have special jails for people like you. Breaking the law in..."

"*Capitán*. We broke no law. We're not going to jail. We have gun licenses..."

"No *señor*, you are wrong. This gun permit expired ninety days from the date of issue at midnight, December 24th. This license expired one hour ago."

"*Capitán*.. When you stopped us that license was still valid and you know it. It expired while we were in your custody. Look, all we were doing is taking a short cut home, a bad choice as it turned out. We are not drug smugglers nor gun runners. We were just down enjoying a hunting weekend, and then all this ."

We argued back and forth for another several hours, and the thought of *mordida* crossed my mind, but what was I going to do, offer him a $10 bribe? No, he had to win something. It was now a matter of face. Sometime back he had realized that we weren't *bandidos*, and the last couple of hours were just an exercise in who's boss in la Rumorosa. Man, if he would have just asked me, I would have told him. Finally, near dawn, we agreed to leave ammo, guns, birds, and gear with him, and we got the van plus our freedom. Timmy was let out, we got in the van, crossed through Tecate uneventfully, and pulled into Huntington Beach at 8 a.m.

His mom met us at the door with "Gee, Timmy, we were starting to really get worried. Is everything okay?"

"Mom, I'll tell you about it later. Say, you got any candy under the tree?"

I drove down three driveways, feeling really badly about being late for Christmas, took some mild heat from the wife, and we opened presents. Timmy remained friendly as ever, but as long as I can recall, he never asked about Baja again.

It was nice being off work for the ten day Christmas vacation. But the unpleasant thought that with the two prime months of duck hunting remaining in Baja, I had no hunting license, no gun permit, and no guns, was disconcerting. Two days later, on a Tuesday, I called Tijuana and set up an appointment with the general, to try and reclaim my guns and hunting license, and to try and get a new gun permit. In the old days this was the routine: get your initial license application through Krasnes Sporting Goods in San Diego, then take it with $30 down to Tijuana for the commanding district general to sign. Today, for whatever reason, this process is so cumbersome and time-consuming that Mexican hunting "outfitters" are the only way you can do this. And the $30 has become $400.

In any event, I was very pleased to get a 10 a.m. appointment with the general on Friday, three days hence. Half an hour before the agreed upon time, I was in the general's outer office, checked in with a slovenly dressed soldier-secretary, and waited. Thinking back, it's always been a bit creepy being in Mexican military garrisons, watching these young appearing kids with no facial hair carelessly slinging their automatic weapons around. Ten o'clock came and went, same for noon, and at one I politely asked if the general had perhaps, ahem, forgotten about me.

"*No señor. El general* is busy. He knows you are here."
In the interim I had watched a procession of military people

parade in and out of the general's office. He must have fielded at least three dozen phone calls, because I could hear his voice occasionally through the door. By 2 p.m. I was hungry, so I announced to the sergeant that I would be going for a bite of lunch.

"That would be unwise, señor. El general will see you soon."

At 4 p.m. the general left, and at 5:30 so did everyone else, save the sergeant. I felt like choking the little jerk, but knew it was better to stay cool.

"Well, looks like I won't be seeing the general today," I said unnecessarily.

"No *señor*, not today."

I left, slightly stung, but forced myself to focus on the facts. I was in a foreign country, where guns and permits are a serious business. I had had a run-in with the authorities, and I was at their mercy. I concentrated on this last thought on the two and a half hour drive back through the border and up to Huntington Beach. Next trip down was going to cost me a vacation day, as Christmas break was now over. My next appointment was set up the following week, and son of a gun, instant replay. Same for the next trip. Boy, the Mexicans were having a field day with me. Each time the secretary was a different one, so the general was just letting me simmer.

By now I had missed three weekends of duck hunting, and was desperate. My fourth trip – actually the second that week – I showed up at 8:30, determined to at least talk to the general. By 10 a.m. there had been a steady procession of people in and out of his office, including a matronly but distinguished looking woman, plus later, two real beauties, probably about my age.

The announcement, "*Señor* Stanton," took me by surprise.

"*El general* will see you now."

This soldier was sloppy with baggy pants and an ill-fitting uniform, showed little if any military bearing, and generally was a carbon copy of the others at the garrison. As I was introduced, I mused what a contrast he was to the general, a silver haired elegant man, with perfectly fitted, immaculately pressed uniform, ramrod straight posture, and intense, piercing eyes. There was no question who was in charge here.

As I stepped forward to shake his hand, he said, "*Es un médico, no?*"

Hand still extended, I responded in Spanish that, "Yes, I was a doctor."

Then as if wracked by pain, he hunched over, leaned on his desk, dropped his head, and dismissed the sergeant. "*Señor,* I have terrible pain. Months now. And, *mire* all these *medicinas,*" at which point he gestured to the twenty-three bottles of pills on the shelf behind him.

"*Me permite?*" I asked as I walked over to look at the drugstore he had been given by six local doctors, with daily worsening of his symptoms. The shelf of drugs included cures for pneumonia, bursitis, athlete's foot, flu, cough, kidney stones, tooth abscess, amebic dysentery, congestive heart failure, sprained back muscles, anxiety, appendicitis, urinary infection, peptic ulcer, clap, and syphilis.

It was an impressive list. I asked which ones he was currently taking, and he surprised me by responding, "*Todos.*" A quick calculation told me he was taking at least nine antibiotics, plus other pills to cover all organ systems of the body. In all, he was taking one hundred and twenty capsules daily. Briefly he told me his symptoms, and I localized the problem to something having to do with the urinary system.

"*Sí,*" he conceded, but he was getting worse, not better. During the conversation we switched alternately from Spanish to English. "Boy," I said. "General, you are so lucky. One of the best, no, the very best urologist in the western United States just so happens to be in practice just across the border, right here in San Diego."

"Quien?"

I thought for a moment, my mind racing. Who in the heck was that urologist at Mercy during my internship? It had been several years now, but I thought I remembered a guy who did urology. Jack. Jack something. You know, when you're a dermatologist in training, you learn the derms, not the GU guys.

"Jack Steele. Absolutely the best urologist in San Diego, general, and one of the two or three best in all the United States. He is known everywhere. He can fix you. Give me a phone and I'll get an appointment for you."

San Diego information did have a Jack Steele, thank God, and yes, he was a urologist. Okay so far. I got the office, talked to his secretary, and after a bit of haranguing and cajoling, set up an appointment for the next day, Wednesday. The general was ready to go now, but I told him that Dr. Steele was an extremely busy man, and that only as a personal favor to me could he see the general tomorrow. One thing was for sure. I had better get hold of Jack Steele tonight before he saw the general next day – just to let him know what was up.

At this point the general reached into his desk, withdrew a personal card, and wrote *"Saludo a mi amigo,* Dr. Larry Stanton." Then he signed it. It looked like the best Mexican insurance I could ever buy. He came over to me, shook my hand, then motioned to the guns, cases, ammo, licenses, permits, all neatly stacked behind me. At an utterance, three men entered the room, loaded up my hunting gear and carried it out to the car.

"Gracias, doctor."

"Buena suerte y buena salud, general," I said as I left.

That night I struck out trying to get Jack Steele. Someone else was on call for him, but he was available tomorrow. Whoa! Available, all right, but not in. Unknownst to me, Dr. Steele was a golfer, and Wednesday was his golf day. So when the general and forty-three military motorcycles, plus two armored personnel carriers and one half-track reached Jack Steele's office, only to find the secretary and not the doctor, they then proceeded to the tenth tee at Singing Hills Country Club, picked him up and escorted him back to his medical office.

Thursday night I managed to finally get through to Dr. Steele. I explained my predicament, what had happened, and how I had involved him. He was gracious, and then gave me the general's followup. Basically he had an epididymitis and a tiny biopsy revealed it to be tuberculous in nature.

"Tuberculosis in the epididymis?" I said in mild shock.

"Oh yes. Very common in Mexican males with previous exposure. They overcome the pulmonary infection, but blood borne mycobacteria frequently end up settling in the epididymis."

Wow! Boy, was I impressed. Good luck on my making that diagnosis when I'd never even heard of such a thing.

"Yes, and we discontinued his twenty-three different medicines, placed him on INH and PAS, and expect a complete cure. His scrotal pain should clear nicely."

I hunted the rest of January, then on into February, and enjoyed each trip more than the one before. It was great to see the guys again, Curran and Palmer. But I have never returned to the U.S. on Christmas eve again, and I definitely have never laid eyes on, been through, or even considered going to la Rumorosa. As for *el general*, I called him several times to check on his progress – he was *always* available – and as for my Mexican insurance card, I had it until several years ago, when somebody bagged my billfold in the San Francisco airport. The money and the billfold I concede; but man-oh-man, what I'd give to have that little Mexican insurance card back.

La Frontera

t had already been a helluva hunt, and we hated to see Lee go, but if he couldn't stay down another five days, that was his business. We had just spent the last three days stalking a flock of Canadian honkers – smartest birds anywhere. After figuring out their flight path into the freshly cut barley field, we had lain in wait in shallow pits covered with *chamiso* and straw for over 3-1/2 hours when *"honk, ca-honk, ca-honk,"* in they came. Naturally, it was the opposite direction from which we expected, so we were just about a half-mile out of range. How did they know? Second sense, I suppose. Anyway, they were majestic coming in to feed, just not in our range.

We all got out of the pits, shook our heads in admiration, and set to the job of how we might get them when they left the field. Of course, they had come in against the wind, and had the wind not shifted half an hour previously, we would have been set up just right. So we loaded up our ammo, guns and the half-dozen field dekes, and began a wide encirclement of their feeding area. They saw us get up, of course, and the sentinel *guia* gave us a few short series of acknowledging *"ca-honk, ca-honk, ca-honks."*

We edged out of the field, crossed through a tree line, then headed way east of the feeding field, so there was no possibility of being seen. Geese are supposed to be able to see only the slightest movement miles off – and we weren't taking that chance after coming up short two days in a row already.

We circled several miles north into the wind, then when once it was firmly at our backs, we headed south, slowly and under good cover. When we could finally see the field, Curran dispersed us – he had the best place, Nold second best and I last – based on degree of hunting experience, I supposed. All I knew was when I heard those geese finally get airborne and start calling, I was 40 yards behind Nold and 80 yards behind Curran. If the geese came our way, the other guys would get a shot, but I wouldn't. Just as we planned, the honkers, now satiated, flew into the wind, gaining elevation. As they came over Curran, he raised his gun to shoot, but realizing they were already too high, dropped the barrel and said, "Don't shoot," causing Lee to drop his gun. They rose higher over me, but I had loaded some double 00 buck just for a chance like this. I put the sight on the lowest, closest bird, then gave him a 15 yard lead, and pulled the trigger as I swung.

"Stanton, God damn you, you idiot," shouted Curran. "Three days we've stalked them, now you shoot and we'll never see them again. You jackass!"

At which point, that lowest, closest bird folded one wing and plummeted straight down into a roughly cultivated field half a mile away. Lupe, who was with us, headed out for the spot, and forty five minutes later, returned with our dinner for that night.

"*Buen tiro, Larri.*"

"Friggin' luck," added Curran, deeply disappointed he wasn't the one to have bragging rights.

That night around the campfire, however, all we could remember was how we had planned our stalks, how we figured out the wind, and how good this roasted goose cooked in coals tasted. It was the stuff campfires were made for. Twice I had to remind the boys who actually shot it, but they preferred to dwell on the stalking and planning aspects. Whatever, we all slept well that night, and were sorry when old Lee had to hit the road next morning. Lee planned to meet up with us again in a month, but Curran and I would be down at least twice more before that.

As Lee drove off, the first dove flights started and it appeared the flight path was quite a bit west of us. There was no road there, so we hoofed it through several fallow fields, and then crossed into a barley field, which had just recently been burned off. First came some pairs, trips, more pairs, then whoa – here came the wolf packs. Large groups of winter birds, 20 to 100 in a pack, seemed to have zeroed in on this burned field. All the chaff and straw had been burned away, leaving only the barley seeds, sometimes charred, for the birds to easily pick over. Whatever, these birds loved it, and we were smack dab in the middle of it.

Curran pulled on a pair and *"bam, blam,"* they both dropped. No sooner had they hit the ground, however, than they were immediately scooped up and gulped down by this mangy, skinny dog.

"You see that?"

"Yeah," I replied, "Nice retrieve." I looked at the dog. There was nothing left of the doves save a few feathers at the angles of his mouth. Where he had come from, gosh only knows, but he had a real eye for downed birds, he was quick, and he was hungry.

Another large group flew over and *"Boom, ba-boom,"* Curran beat me to the shot again, with another double falling out of the sky. The dog nailed the first dove before it hit the ground, and the second was dinner a heartbeat afterwards.

"I'm gonna kill that fucking dog. If he makes even so much as a glance towards any other birds I shoot, he's dead."

"C'mon Curran, settle down, it's just a few doves, we're not starving, and the dog's hungry. A triple came over the trees and once again Curran beat me to the draw.

"*Boom. Boom.*"

"Nice shootin'," as a pair hit the deck.

The dog, who had been watching also, had the first bird in his mouth, and was about to pick up the second when Curran yelled, "Hold it, you shit can." At which point the dog dropped the bird in his mouth, turned to face Curran and gave out a mean snarl, "*Grrrr*," then made a few menacing steps towards Curran...

There was no hesitation, just a "*Boom, boom,*" and the dog dropped dead in his tracks.

"Jesus Mike! What'd ya go and do that for?"

From the far corner of the field, a little Mexican boy came running towards us crying, "*Perro, perro.*" He came up to his dog, and with tears in his eyes, asked, "*porque señior? Porque ?*"

Curran just shrugged, and laughed as we moved on. "Good shootin', huh?"

"Yeah Mike, nice job."

This was another side of Curran – the mean side – and he could be like that. I kinda lost my desire to hunt after that and wandered on back to camp. Curran stayed out and when he came back to camp later that afternoon, he had his limit of 50 doves. Of course, that didn't count the 6 birds the dog ate – nor the dog.

The day's events kinda got me thinking – thinking about Curran, how I had met him, and why I enjoyed his company. He was more than just a convenient hunting partner – although there certainly was some truth to that. No, Curran was interesting to be around. He had great hunting stories, was good around the cook fire, helped split up the workload around camp, and . . .the boy could hunt. How I had met him went back a few years to opening day of duck season. I had been down dove hunting the previous three weekends, but every Sunday I had devoted to building the best camouflaged, best built, best placed blind you could make, in the middle of Duarte pond. Each week I had checked the flight pattern of the ducks, and it didn't matter if the wind was from the north, east, south or west. The blind was situated about half a mile from the north shore, and was in the natural flight path regardless of wind direction.

So three weeks before the season I had begun hauling brush, twigs, and sticks out to this site, and by the third week had a respectable blind to show for it. The work was hard because every bit of brush had to be carried half a mile through the mud. The Friday before opener, however, I had my boat and pulled it through the mud, loaded down with brush and cover. The last thing Friday night, I pulled the boat out one last trip and carefully set out four dozen decoys in just the right pattern: two "U"-shaped spreads which enticed the birds to land within the arms of the "U". I finished by moonlight that Friday, and well-satisfied with my work, pulled the boat back to the north shore, then through the brush covered canals, and finally back to the base camp.

First thing next morning, I was up and in the water at 3:30. I pulled the boat loaded with ammo, food, and water through the canals, and then hid the boat in the north shoreline.

I took enough ammo for the day, plus the Beretta, eats and a few drinks. The moon was down by then, so I had to travel more by feel and sense than sight. At this time in the morning, if I took the wrong heading and walked due south, I could miss my blind by a mile or more. So I eased on, feeling for my footprints from previous trips in the mud below the shallow water. I reached the blind half an hour before first light, but never saw the blind or my dekes until I was within ten feet of it. I admired my work and the setting of the dekes; it was a thing of beauty – for a duck hunter, that is. As I stepped into the blind, I caught the glint of a gun barrel in the starlight. Impossible! I had no gun out here. "Hey, how about a Metribud?" came out of the darkness.

"Who in the hell are you and what in the name of God

do you think you're doing in my blind, you dickweed?" I was trying to put the best face on things.

"Well, it looked like a good spot, right in the middle of the flyway, no matter what the direction of the wind, good blind, and I figured you'd need help killing all these birds. Also, I watched you build this mother over the last three weeks, and you did it just right."

"It never occurred to you to offer a hand?"

"Nah, it looked like you had everything under control. Besides, I was huntin'."

"Well, my name's Stanton, and I'll take the beer."

"Curran. Mike Curran."

And we didn't say another word until first light. There were birds working to the southwest, but they had no interest in us. A *"whoosh, whoosh, whooosh, whooooosh,"* from behind let us know it was time. They had spotted our dekes, but coming in from out of the dark, ducks are really tough to spot. Boy, if this would just hold for another few minutes, we were in. Then a flight from the middle of the pond turned on a dime and headed straight in, silhouetted perfectly against the dawn.

"I'll tell you when." said Curran. He had spotted them also. "On three. One, two, *blam, blam, ba-bam, bam..*" A triple.

"You shithead. I thought we were gonna wait."

While he reloaded, another flight circled and wings locked, sailed in. *"Boom, baboom, boom, boom..*"

"Well, there's four more." A quadruple. Curran was impressed. And so it went through the first hour of dawn. Flight after flight, singles, doubles, trips, to twenty or more – in they came. In the smaller flights we didn't let many get away. It was spectacular shooting, with never more than 15 to 20 minutes between flights. At sun up, the situation changed. Now, as well camouflaged as it was, our blind stuck out like a sore thumb. We collapsed the top half of it down on ourselves, giving us a lower profile, and now depended upon our sprig whistles to get the ducks to come look us over. I was good on the sprig whistle. Real good. But Curran was better. Between us we had stereo-phonic duck whistles, and let me tell you, there is nothing more exciting in hunting than calling in a flight of sprig from half a mile up, and watching them wiffle straight down into the dekes. It's almost like watching a minicy-clone funnel of ducks, feet extended, drop straight out of the sky. When they come in like that, they drop like stones, and the shooting is fast, real fast. We piled 'em up, and somewhere near mid-morning Curran said we had a limit. Fifty each. The possession laws had increased this year in Baja, but I had forgotten. Also I'd lost count.

So we unloaded, and still camouflaged, proceeded to call in hundreds more ducks over the next three hours. Not only pintail whistle. Gadwall, widgeon, and teal, all can whistle, and we called 'em in by the droves. As much fun as the hunting had been, this was better. Sometimes we'd end up with a couple hundred birds in our dekes, which would all get up and fly away at the sound of a cold Bud being opened. Curran knew when to call and when not. Since I had learned that only by painful trial and error, it told me he was really a seasoned hunter, plus being a crack shot.

We finally called it quits, hauled in the birds, and only then did we begin to talk. Turned out, he was from San Diego, also. He was in the Navy, had been in the U.D.T. in Vietnam, and now was doing a residency in radiology. We hit it off great, especially when I found out he knew how to cook. That evening he cooked up Ducks Baja (also known as Ducks Curran) and started what came to be a tradition when hunting in Baja. Hunt hard, eat well. We breasted out eight birds, diced the breasts, and sauteed them in butter. Next we sauteed mushrooms and onions, then added cut up bell peppers, garlic salt and pepper. We let this simmer half an hour then added burgundy, simmered another half hour, then served it over a bed of rice. Talk about delicious!

And so it went with Curran – master chef one moment,

dog killer the next. One thing about hunting with Mike. He was always unpredictable. You were never quite sure exactly what was going to happen next.

We put the dog hunt day behind us and next morning set out for a new area near Zacatecas, a mud hut *ejido* with mud roads, muddy water, muddy everything. Lupe had said he had seen several good coveys of quail nearby, and off we headed. Generally, when quail hunting in new areas, we would slowly drive by likely fields – ie, barley fields which had been recently harvested. We would not hunt a field unless we had actually seen a bird in the field, or as usually happens, near the edge of the field. Either from careless irrigation or a serious rain, the mudded-up roads were passable, but just barely. By noon we had seen exactly nothing, and both Curran and I were anxious to get out, stretch our legs, and run down some quail. The only stretching we did was back at Zacatecas, when we got out at an adobe hut that had two tables and ten Mexicans sitting around them.

"*Lonche,*" announced Lupe.

Well, I didn't see anything that looked remotely like lunch, but boy, did they have the Tecate – in quarts, and it was cold. So we had "*lonche,*" piled back in the Chili Relleño and headed out again, checking likely fields for signs of quail. It was late afternoon before we got into 'em, and then, oh, brother . . . Actually all the fields we checked *looked* good; but the birds were where they were, and if you could spot one, usually there was an entire covey. It happened just a couple miles south of Zacatecas, in cover just ideal for hunting. There were some cottonwood trees, but mainly the brush was three to four feet high, interspersed with open ground; the shooting was two to three up, fold two, wait for the next group. They held exceptionally well, and even without a dog, we retrieved all but two. The big problem with desert quail is that they normally bunch up, then after one shot, they run like rabbits. But not this day. No, we put on a clinic on how to hunt quail, covering probably eight to ten miles from when we left the truck. Lupe followed us at a discreet distance in the truck, so we didn't have to walk the eight miles back to the vehicle. When it was all said and done, we had a limit of 15 birds each, plus the dozen we had shot earlier in the week.

That night I cooked up fried quail in olive oil, floured first, then seasoned with rosemary and thyme. It's a simple recipe, but still is my very favorite for both white meat birds, quail and pheasant. To accompany this feast, I intermittently cooked quesadillas in the hot oil, adding shredded cheddar and green tomatillo sauce just before flipping the tortillas over. Add some ice cold Zacatecas Tecate, and friend, you have a gourmet feast. We ate until Curran finally said "quit" and it was then I noticed he had floured all 30 of our quail.

"What'd you do that for," I asked.

"Well, you know that damn new regulation the U.S.D.A. has, they won't let us bring any uncooked gallinaceous birds (pheasant, quail) back into the states unless they're cooked."

"You're kidding?"

"No. Happened two weeks ago to Joe Bruce and Palmer. Made 'em take the birds back across the border and cook 'em before they could re-enter the U.S."

La frontera translates as the border, but sometimes these Einsteins at the border crossing made it seem more like the wild west *frontier*.

"So you're gonna cook 'em all tonight?"

"Nah, just flour 'em up and in a zip lock bag they'll look like they're cooked. You know those U.S.D.A. guys don't like to get their hands dirty."

"Boy, that's not my experience. When old Les came across the border with a dove stashed inside a quail, the quail stuck inside a teal, and the teal stuck inside a sprig . . . man, they caught onto that one quick. Fined him $1500, right on the spot."

"Yeah, well we'll see what happens tomorrow," and

with that, Curran zipped up his down bag, and was dead asleep.

I lay awake for some time, reliving the day's hunt. Last night I was depressed over the dog; tonight I was elated over finally getting a limit of desert quail. But that's the way things were with Curran – mercurial.

The stars in Baja aren't any more numerous than they are up here in California. I know that the millions of city and urban lights make the stars seem *relatively* fewer. But if you could have seen the stars this one night, you'd swear there were more stars in the Baja sky. That's probably what I love about it though. The beauty is so pristine that it almost makes you ache; barren desert, the same. You know, there are thousands of areas down in Baja that no person has ever set foot on, or in some cases, even seen. That's the Baja I love, and I fervently hope that whatever development the Mexicans, Gringos, Japanese or whoever do, they will not spoil this magnificent land. With these thoughts rattling through my head, I dropped off to sleep beneath a truly wondrous sky.

Next morning we made a feeble attempt at one last dove hunt, but I really think it was just to avoid the inevitable – packing up and heading for home. We said our goodbyes at Lupe's, and headed for *la frontera*. The trip back was slow, as early afternoons usually are at the border crossing. Lots of trucks overheated in line, which necessitated either helping push them across, or changing lanes in front of very impatient drivers. From the time we got in line until we were actually at the Customs station took two and a half hours. Not as long as it could have been, but maddening none the less.

"Both American citizens?"

We nodded.

"How far down you been?"

"Mexicali valley."

"What were you doing down there?"

Dressed in hunting gear, sporting six day's worth of

beard, and with bird blood smeared all over the sleeves of our hunting shirts, one was almost tempted to say "getting married," or something asinine as that. But these boys didn't like to mess around, and would have your vehicle dismantled in a heartbeat if you smarted off to them. So we just said, "Been hunting."

"Okay. You know where to go for secondary inspection."

And with that we drove over to one of the five slots Customs and the Department of Agriculture had for just the purpose of examining birds, checking limits, and investigating for smuggled booze, or sometimes if they were lucky, drugs. I was thinking about the last time through, when Danny had smarted off to the Customs official, and they literally took every detachable item out of my van and left it in a pile on the asphalt. It took us nearly two hours to put it all back together. No, you didn't screw with these guys. They *always* had the last and only laugh.

The guy who came over to our truck was young, curly haired, rather short, and was packing a big old .45 Colt on his hip. We got out to fill out our game declarations, and this customs guy starts nosing through our stuff.

"Looks like you've been hunting," he said non-committally.

"Yep, that's what these game 'dekes' are for," offered Curran. Maybe not quite as nice as he could have said it; maybe there was just a hint of derision in his voice.

"Smart ass, huh? Let's see your birds."

Ducks first, I took out the zip locked bags of two each, which he demanded be removed from the bags.

"What for?" I inquired.

"I wanna see that they're feathered, gutted and have one wing with feathers on it for identification."

"You can't see that through the zip lock bag?" I asked.

"You want to look, go ahead. Take 'em out of the bag yourself," sneered Curran. "*We* don't have to take 'em out of the bag. All *we* have to do is declare 'em."

43

"Oh boy, we're in it now," I thought.

This guy looked at Curran, took a step back, then remembered who was in charge here.

"Okay, what else you got?"

I produced five packs of ten doves each for me, then for Curran, which he made some attempt at counting, yet managing not to get any portion of his freshly pressed, white shirt dirty.

"It says on here 15 quail each. Let's see those."

Again, I went to the ice chest and pulled out the 6 packs of 5 each.

"They're not cooked," he challenged.

"Yeah, they are," answered Curran.

"Open 'em up."

Curran handed him the bag. "You want to see 'em, you open 'em up."

"These birds aren't cooked. You can't cross the border. You'll have to go back – to the end of the line. You can't come into the United States with uncooked quail. These birds carry Newcastle Disease, a disease that devastates the poultry industry. My counterpart with the U.S.D.A. just sent someone back across yesterday, because his birds weren't cooked either." This guy was lovin' it. He had us and he was going to stick it in and break it off.

"Look, you fucking moron. It's true that quail and pheasant are gallinaceous birds, just like chickens. But there has never been a documented case of Newcastle Disease transmitted to chickens by either pheasants or quail."

"You're going to have to go back. You have to go back across the border and cook these birds, or you can't enter the United States."

At which point Curran gave him a long look, got up on the tailgate of the Chili Relleño, went inside, and hit the compressed air canisters, which popped the top up to standing height.

"What are you doing?"

44

Curran ignored him, brought out the propane cook-stove, asked the guy for a match, then lit 'er up with a Bic lighter before he could answer.

"Put that fire out! You can't cook here. This is an inspection area."

Out came the skillet and oil, and in went the birds. Curran retreated back inside, then re-appeared several minutes later with two gin and tonics over ice. "Want one?" he offered to the *aduana*.

"You can't do this. You can't cook on government property, you can't drink alcohol on these premises, you can't...." and he backed away, hand on his .45, to the security of his brother officers, who by now had taken an interest in the goings on in space four. They huddled for several minutes before he came back. The good news was that he was alone and had his pistol in his holster. There had been a serious amount of head shaking over there, and the question must have been, "were we within our rights to cook the quail at the border?" Obviously, there was no code specifically addressing this issue, so they had blinked.

"You've got exactly five minutes to turn off that fire, put down those drinks, and get back across the border," he screamed, the veins on his neck standing out.

"Or what, asshole?" taunted Curran, as he threw three more quail in the pan. We proceeded to eat the just-cooked quail, two apiece, washed 'em down with another gin and tonic, and settled back to enjoy ourselves.

"Three minutes."

"Okay, your five minutes are up. You're history." At which point he unholstered his gun, but carefully didn't point it at us. "C'mon, out. Out you go. Back across the border."

Curran looked down at him and said, "You want a gin and tonic? Quail are great. Have one."

This guy was in over his head, but just didn't know it. He'd be the *last* guy in the world Curran would be afraid of. His voice quivered just a hint when he pleaded, "You guys can't do this. This is government property. This is illegal. This is . . ."

"You show me where it's illegal, little man."

It was the ultimate nutter. Curran had him by the *cojones* and wouldn't let go now. I noticed some of his buddies were starting to whisper, and even saw a couple smiles; one guy laughed, but was quickly silenced.

In the meantime, our escapade had backed up the secondary inspection line so that now *no one* was effectively getting through the border. And we had 20% of the game inspection area taken up. What a circus! As motorists finally drove by and saw what was the hold up, they would shoot us the finger and offer certain pleasantries. Curran was magnanimous with a wave, a raised glass in salute, and then down the hatch.

Between us we ate all 30 quail, unceremoniously throwing the bones outside the truck; cooking flour and oil were spilled onto cement with equal abandon. Once the Customs inspector came back and screamed we'd have to pick up every bone, clean up every bit of spilled oil and speck of flour.

Curran just laughed, broke out some tortillas, and cooked up some quesadillas. He sent me over to where the Customs inspectors were standing, to offer them some; when they refused, I asked if I could take their picture. The little man screeched "*No!* This is government property and you can't take any pictures of it."

From there on, it was just a matter or prolonging the agony. The Customs guy was bewildered, befuddled, and discombobulated. He finally pleaded with us to finish up and just move on, but Curran made a point of delaying our departure as long as he could. He cleaned out the inside of the truck, took our guns apart and recleaned them, re-rolled his bed roll – on and on. Near dusk, some six and a half hours after we had first entered Customs, it was time to move on. We had one last gin and tonic, put her in gear, and drove on into Calexico. At the first left we headed out of town, pulled over, popped the top, and slept off the booze. Early next morning we were back in San Diego already planning our trip next weekend. It took considerable effort, but finally I convinced Mike to go on a quail hunt below Tecate. The Mexicali portal of entry would still be a tad dicey for us, just one week later; they certainly would not have forgotten us, so no point in looking for trouble. We switched to the Dodge van for the next 6 weeks, and steered well clear of the Mexicali frontera. Some years later when I was checking my game through the Mexicali Customs and U.S.D.A. boys, an inspector asked if I was the same guy who some years back had cooked his quail in the inspection area and tied up the border traffic for hours. I just looked at him and shook my head.

"No. No, musta' been somebody else."

"But you look familiar though."

"Yeah, well I've been through here quite a bit over the years."

Chubasco

otoring down the canal like this was to me basically what hunting was all about. Three-thirty in the morning, freezing cold, with your three buddies, boat packed with decoys, *chamiso* close on both sides, a beautiful starlit night, and the steady *"hmm"* of the 10 h.p. Mericruiser – these were the things that I came down here for. This year, the water was way up, so you really had to know these canals; if you chose the wrong one, frequently it would dead end, resulting in time-consuming and laborious backtracking; more importantly, it usually meant you would be late for the shoot. So we knew the canals: dozens of 'em, where they went, where the short cuts were, and in times of changing water level, how deep they were. This early morning trip out was my favorite part, with small tamarack leaning over the canal, sometimes obscuring the sky. But generally, on the long ride out, one could contemplate the universe, the magnificence of the Milky Way, just anything; they tended to be great thoughts, much as you'd have if viewing a Great Master's painting, the Grand Canyon, or some other awe-inspiring sight. We were all caught up in it, each lost in his own reverie.

Curran's motor had not started, so all four of us had piled into my Valco. With all this gear and twelve sacks of decoys, my little duck boat was riding low in the water –

too low, as I had pointed out before I added my weight to the already overloaded boat. For Curran it was no big deal; he just wanted to get going. Asher, Mike, and Nold were all in the stern or mid seats; to balance the boat, I was spread-eagled over the decoy sacks in the bow, lying on my back. All I could think about were those beautiful twinkling stars. I could see Venus, Mars . . . Oh, God that's cold! "Aaargghh," I screamed, as the boat nosed under the water and I was instantly submerged, except for my face.

Immediately I sprang upright, came straight out of the water, and reached around for the guns to keep them from getting wet. Curran had already jumped out and was holding the motor to prevent it from going under. Nold was a little slower and so he just floundered in the brackish water. Man it was cold! Just the brief instant I went under was going to make this a memorable, if not regrettable, morning. Asher was nimble and had jumped off the deke sacks, standing up in the canal, but dry.

"Give me a hand, Asher," demanded Curran. Asher took one step, found a submerged tree stump and fell head-first into the icy cold water. As Asher composed himself, he eased back to Curran, then undid the transom clamps. Curran had the engine safely out of the water, so all we had to do was right the boat and we'd be going again. First, the deke bags were removed; same went for the ammo boxes. We righted the boat, piled gear, motor and ourselves back in and were off. I noticed the sky wasn't quite so beautiful when it was 4 a.m., you were wet head to toe, and shivering for all you were worth. We motored more slowly now; we didn't want to sink her twice. Again we were watching the sky when suddenly, over the western horizon, a huge explosion of green light lit the sky clear as a bell over San Diego, 120 miles away.

"Wow, what was *THAT?*" we all asked in unison. Speculation ranged from an airburst nuclear explosion, to re-entry of a satellite or space vehicle. Whatever it was, the eerie green-yellow glow lasted some time, and briefly lit up the sky for hundreds of miles around. When there was no other blast farther north over Los Angeles, we figured all was well, that there was no nuclear attack – probably just a re-entry vehicle – and got back to the business at hand . . . hunting.

We would try the middle of the pond, as it appeared to be the focal point for most of the duck flights. Cover was sparse to non-existent, so we put out all twelve dozen decoys, then hunched down in the dekes with camouflage netting over our heads. At first light just when the first group deked in, Curran raised up to shoot, stumbled over something and took a header. Only the gun stayed dry. It is a peculiar sight to see a guy completely underwater, his hunting cap floating away, but with one upraised arm holding his gun aloft. Actually, we all learned this fairly quickly down here. If your shotgun goes under in this brackish water, it is ruined and your hunt for the season is over. The Mexican government won't let you register another gun during hunting season.

With Curran wet, we were all on even footing. Everyone was cold and damp; some of us had just started a bit earlier than others. After the first sprig flight which Curran had just flared, we saw thousands more ducks, but they all landed well outside our decoys. Our camouflage netting was a great idea, but it didn't fool the ducks. By nine o'clock the writing was on the wall; there would be no ducks shot today – at least not by the likes of us. No, what was needed was lots more decoys, a bona fide blind, and about twenty drones to build it. We were talking about a major undertaking here, since the shoreline was at least a mile away in each direction. We discussed it, and then tired, cold and hungry, picked up the dekes and headed in.

A huge batch of *huevos rancheros* with extra chiles was just the ticket to get everyone going again; or maybe it was the quart bottles of Tecate. Who knows? Whichever, after breakfast we were down to two hunters: Curran and me. The wind hadn't picked up and it was a remarkably clear day, so we piled in the van and set out for whatever we might encounter. We were looking for quail, but if a pheasant happened to make the mistake of getting up, so much the better. We tried Zacatecas, driving past endless rows of barley, but there was nary a sign. Sometime in the morning we crossed over into Sonora. The dirt roads are not on a map, and only a native would know which of the two states, Sonora or Baja, one might be in. Up by the dusty little *ejido* of Luis B. Encinas we found a small covey, but the quail got into big brush so fast that it was pointless to spend time on them. Hunting quail in closely packed mesquite is virtually impossible. We had all done it, but it is more for exercise than anything else.

Heading north, we circled around Coahuila in some promising pheasant areas, but the *chamiso* was thick. Without dogs, we would be unlikely to scare up a rooster. Finally, we re-crossed the Colorado, on the only bridge south of the border. It served as both a car and train bridge, and boasted one lane, with asphalt poured right up to the train tracks. Usually there was a signal boy, night or day, but they were terribly unreliable. Before crossing, you looked and listened for a train, and if none, you skedaddled across the bridge. That is, of course, unless some yo-yo on the other side got on at the same time. In that case, whoever got to the center first had the right of way, and the other guy had to back up. It sounds like a crazy system, but the locals make it work.

We hit Sombrerete and headed north towards some citrus groves and pumpkin fields. This year they also had some fine asparagus, but it was damp, making walking through it a real chore.

"Can't say it isn't pretty, can you Curran?"

"Nope, but darn it, I had my sights set on some quail."

We had been driving for some four hours now, and Curran, who never seemed to get hungry, suggested we stop and have lunch. That was an unusual request from him, but it sure suited me just fine.

"What'd you throw in for lunch?" I asked, as Curran opened the ice chest.

The *"pop"* told me; it would be a quart bottle of Tecate each for *lonche*. "Jeez, Mike, you spent a lot of time on this. Tastes great." As we leaned up against the van in the afternoon sun, cold Tecates in hand, it occurred to me what heaven must be like. We were there already.

"Mike, what's that up there in the road?"

"You mean out there in the middle of nowhere, with no cover around for two miles?"

"It's gotta be quail, doesn't it?"

"Load up." And off we went.

We left the van where it was, and headed north, each about fifty yards off the road. The birds saw us but were intent on eating something in the middle of the road. At fifty yards, they broke and headed for some short, sparse, *chamiso*.

"Stanton, are you thinking what I'm thinking? How many shells you got?"

"Yeah, we couldn't have *put* them in a better place; and I have enough."

We closed the gap to twenty yards between us, and set off toward the chamiso at a regular but unhurried pace. Those birds were going to hold and we were in for some sensational quail shooting. Right on key, fifteen yards from the first bush, five quail exploded. *"Bam, Bam, bam-bam, blam."* Five shots and four birds went down. Curran and I looked at each other knowingly as we retrieved our birds. Next bush, out came three; I bagged the two on my side, and Curran got his. Next bush, out came six and we dropped 'em all, but one was just clipped and flew a hundred yards out in the field. Curran ran out and retrieved it, as I picked up the others, and we were off. The birds held tight, as they faced the prospect of a very barren and open field on all sides of them.

We hunted the *chamiso* for an hour and never kicked up more than six birds at once. It was a quail hunter's dream. The fact was, it happened rarely, if ever. When we finally kicked the last pair out of the last bush, we looked at each other and just shook our heads. We wouldn't do this again anytime soon . . . maybe never.

Back on the road we stopped to see what these birds had wanted so badly. *Ajojolí!* Sesame seed. They had paid a dear price for it. We put the game bags in back and broke out the Tecates; part was in celebration, and part was just plain old thirst. Man, it cut the dust like no other thing could down here. Besides, as Curran said, he was hungry.

We got back to camp at dusk, and started cleaning birds for tonight's dinner. Curran had done a count; we had twenty each, a two day possession limit. It all evened out, because the day before we had gotten skunked. We cleaned the birds from my game bag, leaving Curran's. Those we'd get to later. Twenty quail would be just right for dinner, quickly fried in olive oil with rosemary and thyme seasoning. Mike would make quesadillas, Mamacita's fresh corn tortillas quick fried with *salsa verde* and grated cheese inside. You'd have to be devoid of taste buds not to like this feast. As the first birds went in the skillet, the boys miraculously returned, and contributed to the meal by opening four ice cold Tecates. Maybe somewhere else in the world someone ate better than we did that night; but you sure couldn't have proven it by us.

Nold and Asher cleaned dishes, Curran stoked the campfire, and I dug out my guitar. I didn't play that much anymore, but Baja just seemed like the right place. Once the sun was down, winter descended on the desert. The temperature went from the 70's down to freezing. Curran had fallen asleep against the broken-down remains of the old adobe house; he had put his game vest on for warmth and was stretched out by the fire. After finishing up my repertoire, I crawled into my bag and was fast asleep.

Next morning we were up at first light, and had a quick dove shoot. There were lots of birds, but they were congregated into "wolf-packs," so every time a group came by, there might be two to five hundred birds per group. We saw several thousand birds, but they flew for only fifteen minutes, and that was it. Curran wanted me to fix fried quail for breakfast, which was just fine by me. "Give me your game vest," I told him.

"Why?"

"Well, we left the birds in your game bag last night, remember?"

"Yeah, but I thought you took 'em out."

"Nope. They're still there."

Curran looked surprised as he reached around and into his game vest. Nothing was there.

"I don't know where they are. I slept by the fire with my game vest last night, and they were in there then."

It was then I remembered getting up for a Tecate pee break in the middle of the night, and I thought I saw two coyotes near the fire, but they quickly ran off. That was unusual, because generally, they'll keep a distance from the fire. I went back over to the adobe house to where Curran had slept, and in the dirt saw two sets of coyote tracks around Curran's sleeping form. Mike took a look also, but neither of us could believe it. The coyotes had cleaned out Mike's bag while he was wearing it. There would be no quail for breakfast . . . at least not for us.

As we said our goodbyes at Lupe's, he was very stern-faced.

"Is no good Larri," began Lupe. *"Chinga. Un injección y Yolanda esta embarazada. Chinga."* Evidently, Lupe had bedded Yolanda, given her one "injection," and now she was pregnant. "Eee, Larri. Is *mucho* bad *suerte.* I have to marry with her, and no *dinero.*"

I nodded my head, sharing in his consternation.

"Is *mucho* bad for *mi familia.* I have to marry with her and no *dinero,* no money."

Curran looked at me and smiled. We were being hit up to foot the bill for a shotgun wedding. Damn. I thought down here if that happened, you just got married, and that was it. But not with Lupe. He needed a wedding for all his and Yolanda's friends, complete with *chili colorado*, Tecate, the whole works.

Mike and I huddled for a few minutes, and finally Curran spoke. "How much?" he asked.

"I dunno Mike – maybe four, five hundred dollars."

Curran was bug-eyed. "Five hundred bucks! You're out of your friggin' mind!"

"Okay Mike. Three hundred." Lupe had us; now we would be the guests of honor, and our wives and kids were invited. Nold and Asher passed, but for Curran and me, it would be expected. Hey, what the heck! How many Mexican weddings had I been to in Baja? Before leaving we entrusted three hundred dollars to Don Emilio, amidst a profusion of *gracias* and thank you's. Next week would be a duck hunt sandwiched around the wedding.

Curran laughed about how we had been skewered, then relapsed into hunting stories on the way home. We were coming back next weekend, and I was excited about the wedding . . . sort of.

Bringing women down would be a drag on many, but Curran's wife loved it. Cindy, Curran's wife, was a real slogger. She was blonde-haired, good looking, smart, a hard worker, *and* she could hunt. What was she doing married to Curran? Well, we all make our mistakes, I guess.

We had come down two days before the wedding, with a hundred pounds of beans and some elk and moose from Curran's last Alaska hunt. We knew Mamacita would put it to good use. Meanwhile, we had a blind to build. Our plan had been to use the boat to haul brush to the center of Duarte pond, build a blind big enough for the boat and the three of us. We would then take off the motor, tie it to a stake, and turn the boat upside down. It was so deep in the middle, that the four feet of water and one and a half feet of mud, made for tough maneuvering.

Two days later on Lupe's wedding day, the blind still wasn't ready, so we planned to work on it until two, then join up with the wedding at five. When we finally left, the blind was perfect. True, it was a bit big, but in two and a half days we had carried enough brush out there to hide a houseboat. We did everything but turn over the boat. We needed it to motor out in the morning, so that would have to wait. We had brought out forty sacks of dekes, which meant 480 decoys around our blind. Man, it was spectacular; this is the way I had read about them doing it in the old days. I couldn't wait; tomorrow couldn't come soon enough!

We got back for the *gran fiesta* just in time. Lupe looked splendid in his rented tan tuxedo. With his hair washed and slicked back, for the first time I realized he was a handsome kid. Yolanda, Don Emilo, Mamacita – they were all beaming. This was a party the likes of which they had never, nor would ever, see again. After the nuptials, I was asked to sing them a song, which embarrassed the life out of me, but I did. It was all in good fun, so I sang "*What Are We Going to Do With the Drunken Sailor.*" Lupe didn't understand most of it, but I assured him it was in keeping with his wedding. We feasted the rest of the night on *chili colorado*, made from tender young goats. Mamacita kept cranking out the fresh tortillas, and of course, there were lots of beans. Tecate helped wash it all down in addition to adding to the general merriment. Sometime later that night we excused ourselves and hit the hay.

We were up at three and gone fifteen minutes later. Everything except the guns was already out there, but we just wanted to be ready before first light. And, there was the little matter of staking up the motor and dumping the boat over . . in the dark, Cindy reminded us.

As we motored through the canals I couldn't help being excited. I had made this very trip hundreds of times, but each time was as exciting as the very first. The anticipation, I suppose, was the key; we had an entirely different approach this time, due to the high water. Last trip we had planned to come three days early, build our blind in *the* best spot, and now we were ready to reap our rewards.

The truth of the matter is that just being down here was reward enough; to try and pull off a hunt such as this was just a bonus.

We had made good time and hit the northern edge of Duarte pond an hour before first light; the starlight would help us find our blind and decoys in the middle of this now very large lake. Curran has a built-in compass, and we motored right to our blind. He jerked the motor off and tied it to the preordained stake in the mud. Next, out came the guns and beer, fruit and sandwiches; we planned to be here for a while. Tipping the boat over turned out to be more of a trick than we had bargained for, as the blind was only as wide as the boat, so we couldn't stand at the sides to tip it over. But that was nothing compared to my surprise when I attempted to stand on the bottom of the now upside down boat.

"Curran, you dickweed. We were supposed to bring my boat, not yours. Try standing on the bottom, dumbshit."

Mike took two steps then slid off the very pronounced v-shaped hull. In the starlight I could see the shrug of his shoulders and the grin on his face, as if to say, "What the heck, that's just the way it is, and I screwed up. Nothing we can do about it now." The plan all along had been to take my Valco, which was the same size, but was flat-bottomed, and would have made for good footing. Standing on his hull and shooting was going to be a trick. More likely than not, we would not be able to stand on his boat at all, which would have been okay, had it not taken up the entire floor of our blind. The thought went through my mind that the odds were beginning to tilt a little more in favor of the ducks.

Most guys probably would have been bent out of shape having a woman along on a hunt like this, but having Cindy along didn't phase me a bit. She was a knowledgeable hunter, knew how to call sprig, had real good eyes for spotting game, she could shoot, and she could take care of herself; additionally she was fun to be around. This isn't a promo for Cindy; rather, it was just the way things were.

Our forty dozen decoys were deployed around the blind in artful fashion. No matter which direction the birds came from, they would be encouraged to settle in within 20 yards of the blind. Everything was perfect, first light was a few minutes off, and it was a great time to just relax a bit, and try and control the anticipation and excitement within. First light came and we heard flight after flight of ducks winging over us, but none made it into our decoys. With a spread like this, that was a bit odd, because 480 dekes at first light is irresistible to ducks winging into the pond after being out feeding all night. As dawn came, I sneaked a glance at Curran, who also seemed a bit puzzled, but his look told me nothing. He seemed to be staring into the tiny whitecaps that had formed on the pond.

"Whitecaps," I wondered. "What the heck are we doing with whitecaps at dawn?" I scanned the sky and caught a glimpse of what appeared to be a darkening cloud covering up the dawn; it was more than that, though, because I could see it extend swiftly both east and west, then rise to the stars to blot out any and all light. Whatever it was, it was impressive and it was happening quickly. Thirty seconds later we stared in awe as we watched four to eight foot waves suddenly leap out of the south end of Duarte, several miles off. In less than a minute they were on us with a wind that howled and tore at the blind. In no time, the blind was completely flattened and Mike and Cindy were struggling to keep the motor from going under. I unloaded the Beretta, handed it to Cindy, and Mike and I tried to raise the boat. It was a chore due to the powerful waves that knocked us over, but after several tries we were finally successful. The inside was one big mud bog, but at least we had her right side up and floating. Next came the motor, and once screwed onto the transom, Curran said "Go retrieve the dekes."

It's hard to imagine sacking up almost 500 decoys, but I gave it a whirl. Two steps out of the blind and a *really* big wave hammered me into the pond; my waders filled with water, and everything from my scalp to my toenails was instantly wet and cold. The temperature must have been in the 30's and with the wind it was freezing. *"Bam, bam "* – another two waves knocked me down, but I had reached the first decoys. The wind and waves had scattered them asunder, so sacking them was out of the question. If I could just tie the weighted lines together, and make one huge floating pod, we could untangle things later.

The wind kept pushing the dekes farther and farther away, so to be able to walk faster, I cut off the bottoms of my waders; but this didn't help either. We'd need the boat and motor to run all these dekes down. As I turned to signal Curran, I saw a most interesting sight indeed. He had taken off all his clothes, and was diving bare-assed naked into the pond, while Cindy stood by steadying the boat. Man, whatever was going on back there was colder than what I was doing, so I plodded on, finding the occasional deke . . . but there were not many. It was incredible; less than five minutes ago we were comfortably settled behind a sturdy blind with forty dozen decoys in front of us. Five minutes later, we're soaked, frozen, our blind is destroyed, Curran's swimming naked, I've recovered eighteen of our 480 dekes, and the lake has turned into a raging sea. How do you figure that? I looked back once or twice at Curran, but he continued diving.

Forty five minutes later, I reached the tules on the east shore, and figured I'd just go pick up the dekes. The wind was still up, but nothing like before; there were still white-caps, but no more eight or even four foot waves. Nor were there any decoys. I walked back into the tules half a mile or so, but found nary a trace. I searched way to the south, then back north, but nothing. I mean, how could you lose thirty-eight and a half dozen decoys? An hour and a half later, I spotted Cindy pulling Curran in the boat. He was huddled under his down coat and vest, obviously trying to get warm. I walked out to them, shaking my head in disbelief.

"How could we lose 450 decoys in Duarte pond?" I asked rhetorically.

"Nothin', huh?"

"Nope, *nada*, nothin'. They're all gone. Curran, what in the name of blazes were you doing back there?"

"First pull on the rope, she fired right up, but when I put her in gear, the prop must have come off. Broke the shear pin, so I tried to dive for it, but no luck."

"Man you look cold. Your lips are blue."

"Yeah. You don't look so great yourself. Hop in."

I did and cut off the rest of my waders. None of my clothes were dry, so there wasn't much point in taking them off. Curran threw me a Bud, opened one himself and pointed Cindy in the direction of camp. She came and got a beer too, then grabbed the rope and started pulling us home. Curran and I sat facing each other with the case of beer between us. Half an hour later I called to Cindy to see if she wanted me to spell her, but Curran answered for her. "Nah, she's doin' fine. Have another beer."

And that's the way we were when an outboard going full tilt flashed by us. There were three duck hunters aboard, and they had one of those cute little pop-up transoms, which allow you to use a big motor in shallow water. They must have passed us doing 40, but when they saw this good looking blonde pulling these two drunks and a case of beer, they whipped around and came back to us.

"Looks like you could use a hand. Want a tow in?"

"Nah," said Curran, "We're fine," and offered them a beer.

They looked at us, the case of Bud, Cindy, and then after looking at each other, they motored off.

"Jeez, Curran. Why did you say that? We've gotta be five miles from camp, and Cindy's been pulling us an hour already."

He threw me another beer, laughed and that was that. We got back three hours later, cold, wet, and tired, unaware of the story that would precede us out of the swamps.

Years later, when I would be talking to other hunters who had also hunted Baja, I would be asked if I ever heard the story about this good looking blonde who had pulled these two drunks and a case of beer out of the Baja swamps in a *chubasco*. And I didn't hear it once either; I heard it while hunting chukar in the central hills of Spain; I heard while hunting pheasant in the highlands of Scotland; and I heard it while hunting geese in the south of Argentina.

Needless to say, Curran and Cindy didn't stay married; somebody said he was just too hard on her... but I've often wondered if he just couldn't compete with her.

La Familia

"Stewart, you okay? Jimmy! Jimmy!"

"Oh, God, my chest and head. Wow! Jeez, what'd we hit?"

"Well, when we came over that last dike, the road that was supposed to be on the other side is now Duarte pond. Hey, don't open that door!"

"Why not?"

"Look. If you open that door we're wet."

Sure enough, we had managed to launch my new Ford van. This was only my second trip down in this baby, and now she was stuck nose first at about a 30° angle into the mud and slop of Duarte pond. The water was only about a foot deep, but at this angle it was over the doors. All our gear from in back had ended up on top of us. The rear end was probably six feet up in the air, and we were going to have to exit through those double doors. Jim was covered with decoys and hunting gear; groceries were on my side and all the bags were broken, the drinking water was leaking out, eggs were a foregone conclusion, and the cans of coke and beer were fizzing and popping. What a mess!

"Let's see if we can unpile everything and get out the back."

Thirty minutes later we were out and had unloaded most of the gear and food, stacking it on the dike.

"That road was here last week, Jim," I offered apologetically.

"You sure you didn't get lost in the dark?" he questioned.

By now it was first light — we were just in time for the first flight.

"Whataya say we deke out around the van?"

"Very funny, Stewart."

Two seconds later a "*whooosh*" almost knocked us over. Frantically, we stumbled pell-mell over one another racing to load up the guns. Hell, we didn't need dekes. We had the yellow Ford van as a beacon for the ducks to fly over. First light along the dikes was always good for teal and a plugged van wasn't gonna spook them at this time of day.

"*Bam. Bam. Ba-blam.*"

"Behind 'em James. Watch this."

"*Boom, boom, baboom.*" Two splashes.

"Double."

"Yep."

"There's more. You take 'em," and Jimmy cut loose with four shots, dropping two cinnamon teal.

"*Boom, boom,*" reverberated through the morning stillness as I decked the other two going away. A few doves flew over the dike and we dropped those also.

"There's breakfast."

"Hey, Larry?"

"Yeah?"

"The van's sinking deeper."

And so it was. When we had climbed out, the windshield was above water, but not now.

"She's goin' down," I added unnecessarily. "I think this shoot's just about over. Got any ideas?"

"We got a shovel."

"Forget it. There's that old Mexican shack back down the schoolhouse road, maybe three or four miles from here. With luck, maybe they'll know who's got a tractor or something."

We left gear piled on the water side of the dike, and if anybody came along, that stuff was history. We took our

guns and a box of ammo each, and headed back down the
dirt road which had led up to the dike. By the way, the
water had in fact come up the preceding week. A one inch
rise in the water level may backflood the delta several
miles at times. We just had been going a bit too fast when
we discovered it.

"How much farther?"

"Don't know Jim. But it can't be too much."

"You know these people?"

"Nah, I've just waved to 'em before."

The tamarack tree just across the canal from their adobe
hut finally appeared, and several miles later we were there.

"*Buenos días.*"

"*Muy buenos días, señor.*"

"*Tenemos una problema..* And I explained to him our
problem.

"*En el agua?*"

"*Si.*"

"*Chingado. Lupe. Lupe, ven aquí.*"

This fat Mexican kid appeared, still half asleep, and his
father quickly explained the problem. When he heard the
improbable story he awoke quickly. Several minutes later
he was gone, running off into the *chamiso.*

"*Sientese, señores.*" And we took a seat. Thus we met
Don Emilio, an emaciated old man, with a withered but
kindly face and genuine hospitality, who has been my
good friend these last 25 years. Silently, appearing from
what must have been the kitchen area of their adobe hut
came Mamacita, a plumpish woman with a pleasant smile
and dark inquisitive eyes. Don Emilio introduced her as "*mi
señora.*" In later years we would fondly call her "Mamacita;"
many, many years later I actually learned her name,
Refugio. Refuge. As we would come to realize in future
years, it was indeed an appropriate name. If things went to
hell in a handbasket, *Refugio* would always figure out a
way to overcome. *Refugio* was the rock in the family, the
steadying hand, the port in the storm. It is the matriarchal

Timmy with his seagull and spoonie. I asked him why he shot the seagull. "Looked like a duck to me" he answered. He was sixteen at the time and hadn't eaten much game, so the spoonie wasn't exactly to his liking. When I cooked up the seagull, however, he had to pass.

All deked out and ready for action. It didn't take much water to bring them in in this arid country. With no rain, we depended on finding a freshly flood-irrigated barley field.

A man's home is his castle and this is where Lupe, his three sisters, parents, cousins and grandfather lived. There was no electricity or water, but boy, could Mamacita cook up some fine frijoles and tortillas in her earthen oven!

Lupe and some desert quail. Lupe could always get us onto birds, but he never understood why we shot them flying. He figured you could sluice 'em better on the ground. The concept of wing shooting seemed ridiculous to him.

These trout came from the middle fork of the Kings River. Asher and Curran are happy anglers. The fishing for these monsters was great, but getting there strapped to the outside of that helicopter scared the pants off me.

I've seen a few quadruples, but hadn't photographed one 'til Curran put on an exhibition.

This is one of our few really successful specklebelly hunts. They came in while three of us were setting out dekes and one guy was taking a leak. Everyone was certain he alone had killed five, but since we only had nine, somebody was exaggerating. Left to right, Brown, Curran, author, Garner.

Palmer and Stanton with a mixed bag of snows and honkers. This was actually just north of the border at a high faluttin' hunting club. Paul kept shooting everyone else's birds and then yelling over to 'em, "Nice shot." They bought it and he must have shot a limit for each blind.

Pancho Villa hasn't returned, but Jimmy Stewart would have fit right in if he had. We got there late that morning, but the ducks did too.

Curran with ringnecks and quail; goats in the background were just plain lucky that day.

nature of many South American families, that when the going gets tough, go see momma. She would allow Don Emilio to do the talking, but the deciding... that was her domain.

She brought all three of us fresh, extra sweet coffee. Only in later years did I realize what a gesture of friendship this was. A pound of coffee for these people cost four days' wages. And sugar wasn't cheap, either. Yet, from the very beginning they were willing to share whatever they had.

We chatted for awhile and within the hour we heard the *"chug-a chug-a chug-a chug-a ching"* of the tractor. Lupe was driving a rusted up old John Deere, with no tires. The metal wheels had virtually no traction but it was better than nothing. Don Emilio got on the tractor with Lupe and we piled several shovels and pick axes on the tool box behind the seat. We thanked Mamacita for the coffee and off we went.

When we finally came to the dike and Lupe first eyed the nosed-in van, he turned to his father and said, *"Chingado! Cabron!"*

Back in those days he was fat and sported a teenager's curly moustache, that made him look like a cross between a comedian and a gangster. *"Es imposible."* he said.

Don Emilio got down, took the shovel, and dug around the van's submerged front end. We joined in, but this stuff was like sticky goo, it weighed a ton, and made our task look, indeed, impossible. Don Emilio was an *irigador* or irrigator, one who lets water from the canals into the various fields to flood irrigate new sown seed. Also if the ditches around the fields broke, Emilio would have to build them back up with his spade. Thus, he was a shovel man, and he worked with this sticky, heavy adobe all the time.

We dug throughout the morning and on into the afternoon, succeeding in digging out around the van. Next we started on the dike. Emilio was actually going to dig an eight foot wide lane through this six foot high, twenty foot wide dike, which had been compacted by years of travel.

Brother, what a job. Lupe, in the meantime, had left on the tractor, and was returning with a flatbed wagonload of Mexican peasants, all equipped with shovels or pick axes. As many as twenty men were working at one time, under Don Emilio's direction. By mid-afternoon we had the dike down and Lupe drove through to hook up the tractor rope to the van. With no tires, the tractor wheels spun, and in no time, joined the van in the water. One of the men took off into the *chamiso* and returned several hours later with eleven mules. Watching all these jackasses getting hooked up was worth the price of admission, but in a flash, they had the tractor out of the swamp. Then, with the mules pulling the tractor and the tractor hooked to the van, they finally unstuck the van, pulled it out of the mud, through the dike, and onto the road.

While we worked on cleaning off the engine, carburetor, air filter, and plugs, the *campesiños* rebuilt the dike. Lupe compacted it with the tractor, and just before dusk it was done. The van fired right up – these Fords were tough – and all of us piled onto the wagon or in the van and headed back to Lupe's.

It was apparent back at the adobe hut that Don Emilio was not only known by all these men, but was respected, as well. Many were relatives, but some were just neighbors who had come at his request to lend a hand. It was hard to know how to thank everybody, so we gave Mamacita all our meat and groceries, and two hours later we all enjoyed a mouth watering spicy stew – *chili colorado* she called it. We washed it down with beers and cokes, then at Don Emilio's offer, bedded down in the van beside their hut.

Next morning I realized we had parked next to an old red Chevy Impala – no tires, no windows, no motor; funny how they would just leave an old junker like that in front of the house. Don Emilio and Mamacita had been up some time, sitting under the thatched roof of the dirt porch, and taking in the warmth from the morning sun. When I emerged from the van, Don Emilio waved me over to sit beside him. *"Sientete aquí, señor."*

I told him in Spanish my name wasn't *señor*, it was Larry. He trilled the double "r's" as is done with all double r's in Spanish and it came out "Larri." So be it. I didn't feel like a Lorenzo – too Italian. No sooner had I taken a seat beside Don Emilio than Mamacita appeared with that marvelous *cafe dulce* – sweet coffee. I thanked her and then we talked about the previous day's events, taking down the dike, sticking the tractor, getting both out with the mules, then the big sheebango last night. *"Que fiesta,"* said Don Emilio, shaking his head and smiling. We enjoyed our coffee, the sun, this serene land in the early morning, and then Don Emilio smiled and said, *"Vamos a platicar."* This was his announcement, then and in the years ahead, that he wished to have a discussion; and it could be about anything. He asked questions like how far away we lived, how long a drive it took from San Clemente to here, how often we came down, what we did for work? It stopped him that first time when I explained I was a doctor, specializing in skin. *"No,"* he said.

"Sí," I responded.

"No es posible."

I guess he had the idea that doctors didn't fish or hunt, were usually in the hospital or office, and certainly didn't hunt in the mud and sleep on the dirt. It took him some getting used to, but gradually he accepted it. He had a very inquisitive mind for someone with no formal education. He had worked in the cotton fields ten hours a day, from the age of six on. Looking at our van, he wondered how much it cost and how long it took to earn a nice vehicle like that. I told him most cars were bought over a perod of three or four years, and that the van had cost $8,000. I translated that into pesos for him and he just slowly shook his head in wonderment. He said it would be impossible for him to own a van such as that because he worked six-and-a-half days per week and earned only $8.00 per week. At that rate, if he spent no money on his family for food, clothing or anything else, he could own this van in twenty years.

But he was not complaining; in addition to working as an *"irigador"* both day and night, he also had a good *negocio* with his forty goats, eight pigs, and, during the years when he could set aside extra money, his two *hectares* of barley. That surprised me. Turned out he had leased two *hectares* (about five acres) around his house, and could make extra money by planting and harvesting it.

Mamacita, meanwhile, took care of the family and worked as a fisherwoman in the swamps. This amounted to setting gill nets in the brackish swamps, and catching *lisa*, or mullet and *bucon*, or salt water bass. These fish were usually sold for 30 cents a kilo or 12 cents a pound. Usually Lupe would help out all months except during the fall, when there was cotton to harvest.

While we were chatting, the time had slipped away and Jimmy had joined us, now into his second cup of coffee. Suddenly the red Impala came to life; the trunk popped up and two little kids crawled sleepily out; next the front door, then the rear doors opened, and out popped two more. Now I got it! The Impala was no longer a car; now it was a bedroom. The four kids came to the table, and talked with Don Emilio; one was his son, Roberto, aged two, and the others were grandchildren. Lupe was oldest at 22, Roberto youngest at two. In between were Hilda, Rita, and my favorite, Ynez. She just happened to be in between my two daughters in age, and over the next ten years, the three of them became good friends. Of course, neither spoke the other's language, but that didn't seem to matter. Kids were kids, and they had fun doing no-matter-what. Of all the children, Ynez was the only one who really was interested in school. Later at age 12, she decided to become an attorney. The last time both my daughters accompanied me to Baja, some five years later, Ynez, at age 17 was married, had two kids with another on the way, and schooling had long gone bye the bye. A shame, really, for if she had held to her dreams, she could have really made a nice life for her family. As it turned out, she fell victim to that trap of so many young people today; marriage, kids, and it's all over. In Mexico, however, it's much harder than in the U.S.

For breakfast, Mamacita offered us freshly made tortillas and beans – I wasn't much used to that for breakfast, but it was the only one they ever had. On rare occasions, there would be an egg; but this was mainly for Lupe and "rare" is used in the exact context of the word. The breakfast was so tasty I couldn't believe it. Never had I eaten freshly made beans with corn tortillas right off the stove. I was curious as to what the kitchen looked like, so when finished, I took my empty plate in and watched, fascinated, as Mamacita and Hilda cooked over the adobe stove, with a steel sheet across it for the hot griddle. I was to be in that kitchen hundreds more times over the coming years, watching *chili colorado, frijoles,* or *tortillas* being made. It doesn't sound like much of a menu, but when meals are that good, who cares. *Chili colorado* was usually made only in our honor, and then only because we offered to buy a *chivo,* or young goat, from Don Emilio; the *chivo* would be freshly butchered, then slowly cooked with chilies in an indescribably wonderful sauce, all day long. But when we weren't there to buy a *chivo* for ten dollars or so, they did not eat meat. Breakfast, lunch and dinner were all the same – *frijoles* and *tortillas.* I once asked Lupe if he ever got tired of the same thing all the time. "Tired of *frijoles* and *tortillas?* Never," he said, looking at me incredulously. And he had a point. If something was truly that good, why would you want anything else? Made me think about all those years when I was forced to learn to like spinach and broccoli. From a nutritional standpoint, however, their limited diet made me wonder how in the world they could exist without milk (although the babies did have this), green vegetables, minerals, and vitamins. Either those things don't mean quite as much as we think they do, or these folks were remarkably hardy. I think it was probably the latter.

One thing kept going through my mind while Don

Emilio and I were talking – next time down here, and all the times thereafter, I vowed to bring down a big sack of rice and beans plus meats, coffee, used shoes and clothing, and maybe even some toys for the kids. It was apparent to even the least observant that these folks needed everything and anything. This was poverty, but they had such a strong family, I don't really think they looked at it that way. The closest Don Emilio every came to complaining about his lot in life was one hot day during dove season.

"Larri, la vida es muy dura." Life is hard... and so it was.

They had an old car. Actually, it was Lupe's, but had been bought with the combined earnings of the family. It was always in need of a radiator, tire, battery, fuel pump, fan belt, or whatever. Incredibly car trouble always happened just the day before Curran and I arrived to hunt. Naturally, next day we'd hit Coahuila with Lupe to find that part. Lupe was a genius with anything mechanical. If the only fuel pump in town was from a '57 Pontiac and it was needed in a '60 Chevy, *"no problema;"* Lupe could not only fix it, he could do it with crossbreeds. It was indeed amazing to look under the hood of and underneath his yellow '58 Ford pick-up: powertrain by Jeep, steering wheel from John Deere tractor, fuel pump from Chevy, carburetor by Dodge, engine from Mercury, and front and back slicks from Coahuila.

Llanteras, or tire shops, are a stock feature of any town in Baja. There are no new tires once you get away from Mexicali or Tijuana. So all these little *ejidos* have these huge tire repositories. Virtually none of the tires have tread, so the longest they could last would be no more than several hundred miles. But that's how 99 percent of Baja gets around – in treadless slicks with a useful life of usually only several weeks to months; it depends on how often they are driven.

But all this aside, it mattered not to Lupe; if it were broken he could fix it, he could adapt. Same with outboard motors. Johnson parts were adapted to fit into an Evinrude.

I know if we did that up here in the U.S., it wouldn't work. But it sure works down there. I guess it all depends on how desperate you are; and they were usually pretty desperate.

In the early years, when Lupe was still in his teens, he played the part of the con man. He was always trying to figure ways to wheedle something out of Curran or me, like the time he managed to convince us to keep our boat and decoys down there, next to his house. He would personally look after it. As I recall, two weeks later we came down late one night to find the boat gone and the decoys, ten dozen of them, eaten up or chewed apart by the goats. The boat was recovered two days later – Mamacita had gotten stranded while fishing, so Lupe went to rescue her in our boat, which was okay, except he neglected to bring it back. We went out to reclaim it next day with the few dekes we had remaining, and actually got into a really fine shoot. Mamacita and Lupe almost always knew where the good duck hunting was because they were always out in the swamps, and they missed very little, if anything. Also, they knew we'd be interested in knowing where the ducks were flying. That was in the good old days, however, before the swamps dried up. They say it was low rainfall, but I really believe the U.S. farmers just sucked the mighty Colorado darn near dry by the time it finally crossed into Baja. And with the water went the hunting – same for fishing.

We finally came to an understanding. If we left the gear down there, it had to be somewhat protected, or we would have to pack it all up and take it home each trip. And as it was a whole lot more convenient to just leave it there, that's what we did.

Camping was another problem. We liked to camp out under the stars, and liked to be away from human sounds. So we camped underneath a huge tamarack tree, just across the canal that ran next to Don Emilio's home. Actually there was an abandoned, fallen-down adobe hut there, with no roof, which served as a wonderful campfire site, or cooksite, whenever we brought more than a couple of fellows down. I often dream of lying under that huge old tamarack, listening to the wind whistling through the limbs, and seeing the brilliant starlit sky above. My daughters have traveled with me countless times over the years to that very spot, listening to and seeing those same wonderful parts of nature. Camping under the tamarack was a compromise in a way, because Mamacita could still see us if she wished, but mainly we were away from the house, kids, cars, what-have-you. Naturally, this in no way kept us from going back across the canal for those wonderful *tortillas* and *frijoles* at lunch, and always at night. I'd go over after dark and chat with Don Emilio. On occasion he would request a medical favor. When we first met, he looked like seventy-two going on a hundred and ten. In fact, he was only fifty-two. But he had ulcer trouble and had to be very careful that he ate no chiles, and drank no beer or hard alcohol. We treated him with antacids successfully, but as soon as he felt better, he would stop them and the symptoms would come right back.

When feeling well, he loved to talk in the evenings. So always on a three day weekend, I managed to save one night and spend it with Don Emilio. We would talk about the current Mexican government, the American government, the value of the peso, the ever increasing cost of food, in a word, everything. His vocabulary was very limited due to his lack of education, so he was extremely easy to understand; likewise, my simple Spanish was easy for him. He was puzzled as to why the Mexican government did not take care of the Indians. They had virtually no welfare system, were denied political representation, and basically were treated as unwanted step-children. I didn't know the answer then, but perhaps it was just that Mexico, in general, was so poor that very little, if anything, could be done – especially in these isolated hinterlands. Basically, the *campesinos*, and in this case, Indians, just had to make do or else.

In later years, Mamacita became a district representative

for the Indians, but there just wasn't a whole lot ever accomplished for the very poor. Still, her political activism was a start. And if you look at Mexico now, it is definitely light years ahead of where it was only a short two decades ago. In their eagerness to improve Baja, I only hope that they don't do it by ruining this last beautiful frontier.

Life at Lupe's was never dull. Goats were eating the barley, coyotes were eating the goats, someone had just cut his toes off, the main road was flooded – there was something every day. Especially there was *el señor*. He was full faced, barrel chested, golden brown, well muscled, and . . . he was 122 years old. I checked with Ripley's Believe It Or Not, and the oldest living person they currently had on record was 118. *El señor* was greatly revered by all, so much so, in fact, that he rated his own bed in the adobe hut. Everyone else, Don Emilio, Mamacita, and usually three or four children, slept in the one large bed in the house. I asked if it was always that way, and Don Emilio assured me, "Si." *El señor*, at age 100, was given his own bedroom, but usually chose to sleep with the rest of the family in the large room. I would guess it had to do with the warmth additional bodies created in wintertime, when the desert can get brutally cold at night. There was a barrel off to one corner of the bedroom and usually Mamacita would get up and add small pieces of wood or (gasp) cut-up chunks of rubber tire. I suppose it's a matter of degree, but I would have to be pretty damn cold to keep warm with a burning rubber tire at night. But in Baja, wood is at a premium, and tires aren't.

During the day time, *el señor* would tend goats, usually finding some nice green field belonging to an absentee landlord to graze the goats. They were healthy Nubians and each breeding season, usually produced twins or triplets, which was seen as especially good fortune. Other times during the day, *el señor* could be seen with a machete or adze, cutting firewood or chopping up old tree roots, which would later end up as firewood.

Don Emilio was his son, so that would mean *el señor* was fifty when he fathered Emilio. Of course, there was also the possibility that he had been older, so we never really knew....until that day when Mamacita brought out *el señor's* most prized possession – his discharge paper from the *Federales*. It was encased in a glass photo holder, and was in remarkably good condition. Proudly, *el señor* showed us that he had been honorably discharged from the *Federales* after thirty years of meritorious service – in 1918. Now if you go back thirty years, it would have been 1888 when he enlisted; assuming he enlisted at age eighteen would mean he was born in 1870. This happened in 1992, so you figure it out.

Conversations were a little harder with him, because he spoke very softly and probably used some Indian words I did not understand. Whenever we were leaving until the next trip down, he always asked for *cartuchos* to keep the coyotes away from the goats at night. Even inside the pens, goats were susceptible to coyote attacks at night. He had an old single shot 20 gauge, which I had seen him shoot some years before. But he was always early to bed and I had a feeling if anybody got up at night and shot at coyotes, it was Mamacita. Imagine just being in the presence of someone 123! His long-term memory was pretty good for stories about Pancho Villa, but his short-term memory was typical for an elder – i.e. short. It was amazing to watch him whack away at *chamiso,* mesquite, or what-have-you, with that razor sharp machete. Far from being dependent on his family, he contributed in a not too minor way. Occasionally he would have a *Tecate* with us, but that was unusual. Sometimes I wondered if he didn't just stroll off with it and caress it, thinking about how good it had tasted in those days gone by. When it came time for dinner, *el señor* was always deferred to, and served first. If there were guests, such as we, adults would eat first, while the children hungrily stood around the table watching us. Once finished, they seated themselves on the now unoccupied benches and ate their *frijoles* and *tortillas* until satiated.

After breakfast or lunch, *el señor* would pick out his favorite bench and then just sit with his face in the sun, looking for all the world like a contented cat. Rarely, if ever, did I see him get in a car and leave the house. His handshake has remained firm throughout all these years, and his well-muscled forearms and upper body are undoubtedly due to chopping firewood. Occasionally, he would tell me a *chiste* or funny story, but usually half way through he got the giggles, and I couldn't understand him through his soft laughter. God, I hope I'm that way when I get to be half his age. His diet was like that of everyone else – *frijoles* and *tortillas*. When we had a *fiesta*, however, and Mamacita made *chili colorado*, he was always served the largest chunk of meat – boneless of course, as he had just one tooth. Mexican families seem to treat their elders just a whole lot better than we Americans do. Funny thing about the family, though. If you were to see Don Emilio and *el señor* sitting next to one another, you'd swear the father was younger than the son. Emilio looked every bit his age and more, and *el señor* didn't. "Age," he said. "Age is what did it. When you get to be as old as I am, there are no worries or cares." He basically ate when he got hungry and slept when tired. "What worry is there in that, *señor?*"

I had no answer.

El Indio

upe, *frijoles*?"

A quick look, a condescending smile, and "No *gracias*, Larri," as if to say "You don't really think that I, a Mexican, would have the slightest interest in your *gringo* beans?"

"Okay Lupe," at which point Curran ladled me a huge plate of scrumptious, steaming hot chili beans. Well, maybe not just beans. This iron pot had simmered at home for two full days to get all the different flavors of antelope tenderloin, home made venison and pork sausage, elk loin, mild red, green and yellow chilis, melt-your-lips hot *jalapenos*, onions, garlic, and of course, *frijoles* – Mexican pinto beans. This creation was enough to make even the most reluctant eater – chili fan or not – want a huge bowlfull.

Indio, who had been out scouting in the starlight, could not help himself, and very casually got downwind of the open chili pot and was hooked. His mouth began to water as he took a seat nearer the fire and looked away. Lupe, by now realizing his mistake said, *"Bueno,* okay Larri – a little bit." Out came his mom's homemade tortillas, and next thing he and Indio were hand-scooping the chili out like vultures after a freshly killed carcass.

"Indio," I said as I proffered another bowl towards him. He took it quickly and with several more tortillas, scarfed it down. Asking if they wanted seconds was unnecessary, as they helped themselves.

"*Cerveza*, Lupe?" and he readily accepted a bottle for each of them, briefly appreciating the "Tecate" label before chugging it down.

"*Es bueno*, Larri."

Curran and I had our second helpings, but still the pot remained half full. Watching us warily, after it became apparent we were satiated, Lupe and Indio attacked the pot and polished off the remainder.

Prior to dinner the green Chili Relleño had been parked precariously, straddling a ravine, so that we could get a somewhat level floorboard on which to sleep. Tomorrow, December 31st, would be the last day of Mexican deer season, and somehow, Curran the finagler had managed to register his .270 Winchester. Mexican authorities ban the transportation of military caliber rifles across the border. Technically the .270 is not military caliber, but certainly it is capable of being used as such. Whatever, Curran had his .270, and tomorrow we would hunt deer.

We had first discussed a deer hunt back in August when we got our licenses. Mexican law allows two guns to be registered and Curran chanced registering just one shotgun – hence no spare if it broke – and the .270. During the first dove hunt in late August, Lupe had mentioned that one of his distant relatives, Indio, lived in the Chocolates, and knew where to find big horn sheep, or *cabrones*, and deer. Desert big horns, of course, are protected from hunting except by special permit, which with outfitters, gear, license, and food, comes to approximately $17,000 to $20,000, depending on the locale. Deer, on the other hand, are relatively plentiful in the mountains, and if you can find water, you will find them.

Until yesterday, we had not heard much more about Indio, and since arriving several days earlier to hunt ducks and quail, had seen neither hide nor hair of him.

"Lupe, are you sure Indio will be here?" I had asked at last night's campfire.

"No te preocupas, Larri. Viene."

And so, as we were speaking, Indio was suddenly squatting beside the fire. Neither Curran nor I had seen him approach; we had heard nothing. He suddenly just materialized, warming himself by the fire. The dozens of times Curran and I had camped alone, we had never been taken unawares by an intruder. But Indio, graceful as a gazelle and quiet as a shadow, had slipped into our camp and we had never heard nor seen a thing. Spooky. One other thing. His tattered cotton shirt revealed a hugely powerful upper body, bull-like, with nary a hint of fat. His face was angular, with the traditional high cheekbones, skin the color of ebony with evidence of weathering, and then the eyes – coal black, hooded, furtively glancing about the camp or at Curran, once at me.

Lupe broke the silence with some unintelligible greeting. Indio grunted but did not speak. We were not introduced, nor acknowledged, but Curran finally asked him about prospects for finding deer the next day. Indio's face remained impassive, until Lupe translated, again in a tongue I did not understand. It suddenly dawned on me that Indio only understood Cucupah, not Spanish. I vaguely recalled Lupe's mother, Refugio, relating in the past how her family had been financially persecuted by the government through the years, because of their Indian heritage.

Indio again grunted and after a brief confab, Lupe told us we were in luck, as there were deer all over the Via de la tres Valles, tomorrow's destination.

As Curran and I peppered Lupe with questions, we suddenly realized Indio was gone. Man, this guy was like a ghost; he could appear, then disappear, at will. I have seen nothing like it before or since.

Dinner finished, Curran cleaned the cast iron bean pot with a wooden scraper, then with a paper towel doused in olive oil. A good wilderness cook *never* cleans his iron pot with soap, water, or steel wool pad. We stoked the fire one more time, as the desert winds howled through camp. Lupe was already down, curled up in his serape and directly underneath the truck's engine, which despite the cold wind, was still radiating heat. Some years later, when I first owned cats, I was to see them do the same thing. Makes sense.

Indio, in short sleeved shirt, remained squatting by the fire, and I asked Lupe if Indio wanted to sleep in the front seat.

"No, Larri, he will sleep on the ground."

Curran and I got in the back of the truck, popped the top and fell dead asleep in our sleeping bags. When I got up to take a leak several hours later, Indio, now lying by the last embers of the fire, watched me with sentinel eyes the entire time, 'til I returned to the truck. The wind was bitter cold and I was shaking so much that it took several minutes to empty my bladder. And yet, there was Indio in short sleeves, lying on the ground. As I went back to sleep I remember thinking, "God, that Indian is tough." I also recall Curran getting up and locking the back door to the camper – something I had never seen him do before. This Viet Nam navy seal, tougher than scrap iron – he was afraid of Indio *also.*

Next morning we were underway at first light, bouncing along over the sand dunes and foothills. If anything the wind had increased, and even with a down coat inside the cab, it was cold. As we drove, we ate the Mexican hunter's breakfast – Tecate, jerky, then another Tecate, more jerky. With the four of us in the cab, steering was next to impossible, but we needed Indio to guide, Lupe to translate, and Curran at the wheel. I sure as heck wasn't riding in back of this frozen, bouncing vehicle. We continued, ever more slowly up into the Chocolates, to the very apex of the foothills, just at the mountain's base. Curran parked the truck at a 45-degree angle, and Lupe blocked all four wheels. It was obvious that when we returned, we would have to back down a considerable distance, for if we attempted turning, the green Chili Relleño would surely topple over. It was now dawn, and Indio had led us to a cut in the mountains, where we would now begin our ascent, *straight up*. It didn't take a genius to know to pack light, carry emergency water, a tin of sardines, minimal ammunition, a down vest that could be removed, and a light weight space blanket in case we had to spend the night. Curran had his .270, I had the 12-gauge Beretta (in case we came across birds), Lupe had his serape, and Indio had his cotton pants and shirt. It was only then that I noticed he was barefoot.

The plan was to scale the mountain, basically straight up, get up on top as soon as possible, then hunt the top. Indio had seen two nice four-point bucks the previous week. The crack in the mountain we were climbing was old time-worn shale, now decomposed and converted to a fine soil in which grew agave, cactus, various grasses, and in spring, high desert flowers. We began the climb in a group and found the going relatively easy the first hour and a half. Lupe, packing about forty extra pounds, was last, with Indio in the lead, Curran right behind, and I in the middle. To this point, footing had been relatively good, but the higher we went, the looser was the mountainside, and for every five steps, we slid back two. I was glad for the gun strap which securely fastened the Beretta to my back – but looking at the terrain, I now wondered why I had brought it.

Thirty minutes later Lupe was done and called a halt. Indio kept going another hundred yards, then seemingly disappeared. Lupe finally got up to us and found a cave back in the mountains with a pool of fresh water, recent Big Horn sheep tracks, and an incredible pair of shed, dekeratinizing sheep horns. Curran guessed they measured some 40 inches around the outside circumference, a fine set by any standard.

After a brief rest, we headed up again, but not before Lupe asked "How much farther?" The reply was not to his liking, so I figured we still had a stout hike ahead of us. As we climbed above the level of the cave, I turned to shout encouragement down to Lupe, who was obviously considering calling it quits. At this point, I noticed the cleft in which we had been climbing, dramatically opened up, and the far wall of the mountainside was now fifty to sixty feet behind us. And there was something else – a brightly painted rock, oblong in shape, some fifty feet in length, fifteen feet in height and width, apparently sitting on a ledge. The painting was a garish yellow and it depicted what appeared to be a snake. The rock had been carved out of the mountainside, the face of which was vertical. I assume the sculptors accomplished this by holding onto ropes from above, but why on earth here? The only place this sculpture/painting could be seen was fifteen to twenty feet above or below where I was clinging to the mountainside.

Lupe had by now caught up with me, and we headed upwards again. Curran and Indio had waited also, but it was apparent they were both chomping at the bit to get to the top. In the next fifty feet the climbing became steeper with no more rock and only brittle shale. Hand holds of grass clumps, weeds, even the base of a cactus, were a must. The way to the top was now guarded by a forest of cactus, agave, and other spring shrubs, and if you slid back down after a short advance, the cactus spines were there to encourage you upwards. Threading my way through the cactus with the shotgun on my back had become a real trick, and again I wondered why I had brought it.

Of course, there was that wild goose chase three years back, when after seeing no geese in three days of goose hunting, Lupe had told me about this place in the mountains where we might find them. With my frustration level running over, I reluctantly agreed, but to hunt geese in these desolate mountains sounded like a half-baked idea at best. Yet that evening we had driven to the Chocolates, due west of the swamps, and at sunset began climbing the mountain. Same as now, it was loose shale, straight up and downright unpromising – or ridiculous – for a goose hunt.

But not wanting to look like a sissy, I followed Lupe. As darkness approached, however, I began to have second thoughts. Was this a setup? Was I going to be attacked by a bunch of his *bandito* friends? What had I gotten myself into?

Then, just as my imagination was about to do me in, Lupe gave me the sign. We were one ridge too far over. Like an idiot, I pretended there really were geese on this mountain cliff and I hunkered down and moved next to him. I peered over the vertical ridge and, lo and behold, Canadian honkers! We were too far away for a shot, but the absurd sight of these majestic birds clinging to a mountainside, cackling up a terrible racket, was just too much for these tired old hunter's eyes to believe. As we watched, more geese piled onto the mountainside, bringing their number to at least four dozen. No wonder we hadn't seen any geese in the swamps. Hell, they were all perched precariously on a darn near vertical mountain cliff. I remember thinking, "I just had to know what they were doing there." I gave Lupe my shotgun and noisily sliding, jumping, leaping and falling, I moved sideways towards them, resulting in some incredibly awkward and hilarious attempts by the geese to become airborne. Some tried to fly straight up but couldn't. Others tried to fly sideways but couldn't. What worked best for them was to head downhill at a fast walk and immediately they would become airborne. By the time I reached their gathering place, it was dark and I found no water, no ledge, no special grass, no grain. Puzzled, I rechecked the areas and could only find that the footing was impossible due to the fineness of the crushed shale. I picked up a handful and then realized that it was minute, perfectly round, and just perfect for a goose's craw. They had flown all the way up this mountain, landed on the vertical, just to gravel up. Tiny gravel such as this is eaten by the geese, goes to their gizzard and then aids in digestion by grinding up whatever grains they had eaten that day. Normally, geese, chickens and ducks will just find some tiny gravel along a roadside or riverbank and "gravel up" there. God only knows what weird quirk in nature had made them forego the easy gravel to fly up into this mountain for the same thing. Maybe today's deer hunt would bring a repeat of what happened three years previously – but I doubted it.

Breaking my reverie, Indio had shouted something down to Lupe, which greatly increased his effort to get up the mountain. From the way Lupe climbed, I could only assume it was some supreme insult. Whatever, we all four charged for the top, non-stop, and 45 minutes later we were in sight of our objective. At this juncture, Curran and Indio took off at a frenetic pace, virtually running up the mountain face, through cactus, not around it, with first one to the top being the winner. Although winded, I pressed on because I wanted to see the finish of this *mano a mano* contest. At the very end, Indio went into overdrive, and beat Curran by a hair. To rub Curran's nose in the defeat, he sprinted fifty paces more into the thick cactus forest on top, then abruptly stopped. Curran waited for me, then together we went to see what had halted Indio so abruptly. Curran unslung his .270, expecting a bedded down deer, but as we approached, there was Indio, one foot firmly on the ground, the other on top of an agave, with the spike sticking neatly three inches through the top of his foot. It was something akin to stepping on a punji stick, I suppose. Curran smiled and then took out his knife, but Indio shook his head. He looked Curran right in the eye, slowly withdrew his foot from the spike, then set off again at a lope through the mountain cactus forest, Curran close at his heels.

We hunted that mountain top 'til darn near sundown. Curran and Indio never stopped, and Indio never complained about the foot with the spike injury. Several times we were on fresh sign, but the deer gave us the slip. Lupe finally called it a day and together we slid down the mountainside in a twentieth the time it had taken to climb it. I did notice that Indio gave no indication of wanting to race Curran down the mountain through the cactus in the dark.

I also remember thinking that had I been in Indio's shoes – or rather barefeet – it would have taken a medivac helicopter to get me off that infernal mountain. And I guarantee there would have been no deer hunt. When we got back to the truck, Indio was gone. Lupe said he would walk home through the desert. Curran, who isn't one to acknowledge a feat, merely raised his eyebrows, got in the truck and we headed back to camp. An hour later, tired and hungry, we both forewent the food and crawled into our sleeping bags. Just before dozing off, I heard Curran mumble, "Son of a bitch, that sucker was tough." And he was.

Mesa Andrade

dunno, Larri. I think it is very *dificil* to hunt *la mesa* with so many hunters." It was a couples hunt, the largest group I had ever hunted with in Baja. Curran, Nold, Asher, Klinger, and John – all with their girl-friends – formed an impressive entourage. Three guys, four tops, are ideal for hunting quail. Including two women hunters, there would be nine of us in all – way too many for a quail hunt, as Lupe had correctly pointed out. As the sun set lower, I finally convinced Lupe it would be okay. Not to worry.

"I dunno, Larri."

But in the end he gave in and we piled into the green Chili Relleño and the deadly Dodge van, and headed east. As usual, the farmers were flood irrigating, and had flooded entire sections of the dirt roads. After backtracking ten miles twice, we came into the low lying desert hills of Mesa Andrade. Unfortunately the detours had made us a bit late, so we would have to hot-foot it once we got going. We travelled a few miles more into the mesa, this strange forbidding place, before Lupe spotted the huge *chamiso* and mesquite patch he had been looking for.

"Is there," he pointed.

I had heard much about Mesa Andrade over the years and had explored quite a bit of it on my own. But these dunes were huge, and wandered endlessly south and east.

I couldn't help recalling the tantalizing stories the old Chinaman at I.V. Liquor had told us. We usually stopped there in Calexico for ice and Mexican auto insurance prior to crossing the border. He loved to cook and his favorite dish was *la grulla,* or sandhill crane. Supposedly there were some hidden springs in the mesa that green head mallards would visit, along with *la grulla.* On two separate occasions I had wandered over these hills for nearly a week, and never saw any sign of cranes or ducks – not to mention water. I even had a friend fly me over the area, but again to no avail. If there were ducks in these dunes, they certainly had nothing to fear from me.

But quail... now that's a different story. Just looking at that *chamiso* with it's partially eaten seeds was proof positive there were quail here. And not just quail, but large, plump desert quail. Looking at the tightly clumped mesquite, however, I knew the hunting would be tough. As we got ready to go, what I saw looked dangerous. Lupe in the lead, would be followed by eight other people, single file, all carrying loaded shotguns. Not knowing how much hunting the two women had done, I made a point of reminding them to keep safeties on and muzzles pointed down at the ground, not at the person ahead of them. Still, the thought of eight people single file through dense *chamiso* and mesquite was disconcerting.

We started out at a rapid clip, and in no time heard the "*cha-ca-qua, cha-ca-qua*" call of the desert quail. Seeing them, however, was another matter. The cover was so dense that unless a bird flushed straight up, we'd never see it. And those beauties were way too smart to do that.

"Lupe, " I asked, "Does this *chamiso* open up, or is it all like this? Hell, we couldn't touch a cap off here if we had to. *No es bueno, Lupe."*

He was breaking brush as fast as he could, but when I spoke, he slowed, held a mesquite branch momentarily, and then let it go. Smack, it smashed right into Curran's unsuspecting face, and he dropped like a head-shot elephant, right at my feet. I saw him go down, but had no idea what had felled him. I bent over and he was clutching his eye, not saying a word, but his face was a frozen grimace of pain.

"Curran, you okay?"

"My eye, my eye. Ohhhh. My eye."

Well, that pretty well localized it, but I couldn't see much. We were deep in mesquite and there were late afternoon shadows making an eye exam impossible. By now the whole troop was around him, so we slung him over our shoulders and headed back toward the Chile Relleño. Since I had been working emergency rooms in Los Angeles for the last three years, I felt most comfortable in doing the exam. But he had his eye squinted shut so tightly in pain reflex that I could not pry it open.

"Anesthesia," I said. "Bring anesthesia."

Old Lee High knew what I meant, and he returned quickly with the Beefeaters.

"Down you go, Curran. Big sip. Now another. Nah, c'mon. Big sip. Chug it."

He took a tiny swallow, then handed the bottle back.

"Damn it Curran. Big swig, like this," and I drained three mouthfuls. He took the bottle back, and followed my example. Then he returned it to me and I repeated the procedure. We did this back and forth until the quart was drained, and I noticed the eye had opened somewhat, though it was really irritated and blood shot.

"Hold him," I told Lee. I pried the eyelid open more, but didn't see anything .

"My contact. My contact is broken into my eye."

This called for another look, but Curran was squinting the eye closed again.

"More anesthesia," I demanded, and here came a bottle of Jack Daniels. We slugged this one down too, and Curran relaxed a bit more.I looked again, but could still see nothing. Lee had reappeared with a pair of tweezers and said, "Let me have a look."

"Hold him."

Curran struggled mightily , but with six of us holding him down, he couldn't move much – until, that is, Lee started picking broken contact plastic out of his cornea. He fought us but succumbed to the gin and bourbon at just about the same time I did. None of the four physicians present had ever seen a shattered contact lens, let alone imbedded in somebody's cornea. Curran was a stalwart, but we hurt him taking out those broken pieces of plastic. Finally, when the eye appeared to be free of broken contact lens, we got some duct tape and wrapped it tightly behind Curran's head and covered his eye. It was quite a sight – grey duct tape wrapped around eye and head, combined with this peculiar staggering gait. He looked like Lee Marvin right out of the movie *Cat Ballou*. We piled Curran into the green Chili Relleño, and I drove. Everyone else got in the Dodge van and followed.

There were a number of dikes and canals we crossed on the way home, but I can recall none of them. According to the witnesses riding behind us, each time we crossed a canal or dike, we were airborne at least five to six seconds. Supposedly, the folks behind us tried to catch us and replace our driver, but at the third to last canal, they were losing ground to us at seventy miles an hour. All I can recall is getting back to camp, opening the door and hitting the dirt face down. It was the same position I awoke from long after dark, some three to four hours later. Everything in my head was spinning but I was cold with just the hunting shirt on. There was some commotion in the pop-up camper, and as I stood at the tailgate, Curran threw old Nold right out of the truck.

"Mike. Take it easy," I said as I put on my ten dollar K-Mart jacket. Curran's one good eye was bloodshot and he was swacked.

"Easy son. Settle down." And with that, he kicked me in the forehead and knocked me out cold. When I awoke sometime after midnight, the coat-arm that had been near the campfire had burned off neatly to the armpit, leaving only the fire retardant lining. I wore that sucker the next two hunting seasons, just as if it were my badge of courage.

When it came time for the dove shoot next morning, neither Curran nor I took the wake up call. I have no idea when the others left, but Curran and I finally got going in the afternoon.

"No wind. Looks good for quail," I offered.

"Yeah."

"Let's do it."

So we set out for Sombrerete, near the safflower field, Curran with his duct tape head dressing and I with my one sleeved coat. We looked so disreputable, that when a Department of Fish and Game warden drove by, he never even gave us a look. We looked like we belonged. Maybe we did.

Estación Coahuila

As we pulled into the farm implement yard, Paul jumped out and yelled, "Domingo!" He was the owner of this tractor and farm machine business, complete with service mechanics, tires, and who knows what else. As businesses go in Mexicali, this was indeed a big one. Paul's black lab jumped out behind him as Domingo came over to welcome us. The two had met several months before, when Paul had been the anesthesiologist for Domingo's gall bladder surgery. When Paul found out that Domingo not only owned the tractor and implement concession in town, but also farmed hundreds of *hectares* in the Mexicali Valley, they became fast friends, and this resulted in Paul being invited to hunt Domingo's fields. He had been down once already this pheasant season, and had murdered them.

Out of the corner of my eye I caught a black shadow stealthily streaking towards us until suddenly *wham*; this big guard Doberman grabbed Paul's lab by the throat and clamped down in a vise-like death grip. The attack took us all by surprise, knocking both Paul and Domingo off their feet. Snowflake was in big trouble and Paul responded with a kick to the Doberman's ribs. Nothing. Then another, and another, and another. Still nothing. Domingo shouted at his dog to stop, but this baby was interested in one thing only . . . killing. Dan came out of the car with a tire iron, which Paul took and beat the Doberman with a dozen times across the head, back, legs and ribs until finally he let go. If that S.O.B. didn't have a fractured skull and a dozen other broken bones, it was a miracle. Snowflake was still alive, but just barely. We made our hasty farewells, then bombed on over to the cornfields.

When we stopped, we were still within Mexicali city limits, and there was city both north and south of us. But this area was a greenbelt of corn, cotton, and barley, and was just primo for pheasants. There was *chamiso* on three sides of the corn, and a once-picked cotton field to the east side. We walked with the rows, back and forth, but it wasn't until about halfway through the field that the first bird got up. "Hen!" Dan shouted, and our guns came down. There was pheasant sign everywhere, and just a bit of dampness in the dirt, like the pheasants seem to prefer. Another pass and this time three cocks got up. Paul nailed one, but Dan and I were in the wrong spots. The next pass, we had a dozen birds get up, and took three. The next pass there were forty birds; the next row more. The closer we got to that once-picked cotton field, the more concentrated the pheasants became, as they knew they were being pushed towards a very open field, and hence they were congregating in the last few rows of corn that offered good cover. When at last we came to the final swing, I could not believe my eyes. Ten birds, twenty, forty, a hundred, another hundred, suddenly broke from tall cover and jumped into the cotton field. It ran about half a mile east, before dead-ending into a raised canal. Dan and Paul ran after the birds, but they sensed death, and were intent on getting out of Dodge. I watched as Dan and Paul closed on them, only to see a solid sheet of birds get up at the far end of the field and sail over the dike. The entire sky filled with a beautiful cinnamon color as the birds jumped up *en masse*. In some forty years of hunting I have never seen a display such as that. Later, back at the truck, as we were cleaning birds, we guessed there were close to four hundred pheasants in that one group. I had no idea they would concentrate like that, and further more, I didn't realize there were that many pheasants in all of Baja. But there were.

Dinner that night was Tecate with fried pheasant, cooked under the tamarack trees at our campsite near Lupe's. I cooked a bunch extra for tomorrow, as somehow I had the premonition we'd need it. We recounted the day's happenings by the campfire 'til late, then all fell asleep under the stars.

I don't recall getting up the next day, but must have as I awoke to the bouncing of the Suburban over the back dirt roads, through Mesa Andrade, and over toward the Huelton canal area. As we sped down the twisting, unmarked desert road, the only thought that kept going through my head was, "These guys are *both* outlaws!" Each would do literally anything in the name of hunting or fishing. Between us we'd had five wives, and I was certain that some of our crazy escapades had contributed to our impermanent marital relationships. Both of these bandits would drop anything at a moment's notice, if there were a hot bite on, or a if a new storm had just driven down some ducks. For better or worse, it was a sad fact that family had to endure in spite of our hunting and fishing obsessions – unfortunately, it applied to all three of us.

"Don't you think we're going a little fast, Paul?" I questioned.

"Nah, I know this trail like the back of my hand." This from a man who had gotten us lost on his family's hundred year old ranch near Springerville, Arizona, several seasons back. As we were wandering for two days through the snowdrifts and mountains back then, I specifically recall Paul stating, "Don't worry, I know this area like the back of my hand." Eerily, I sensed we were about to get into some *big* trouble.

As usual, we had left our camp site late and had to make up time by increasing our speed. In the wilderness, and especially in the desert, that can be a very false economy.

As we blazed along in the starlight, I guessed we were near the swamps formed by the Huelton canal. They seemed so incongruous out here in the middle of the desert, but in Baja, one gets used to stark contrasts such as this. The trail we were following had been made by Mexican fishermen who had built some lean-to fishing huts near the water's edge, and used these as base camps for their gill netting operations. It never ceased to amaze me how these Mexicans could look at a mud slough, desert, or whatever, and immediately figure out a way to drive through it.

"Hour to first light, guys," I said unnecessarily; they already knew it.

"There's that clump of tamarack. We're close," added Paul.

"Palmer, you'd best go a little easy through here or we're not only going to be hunting in the swamp, we're going to be parked there."

"Yeah, yeah."

The water was now visible off to the left, and it was curious how it had invaded the desert in isolated arms and small potholes, extending from the larger swamp further beyond.

"Careful here, Paul."

"Yep." And with that, there was a splash followed by three heads banging into the windshield.

"Damn." It was Paul.

"Everybody okay?"

A quick look around the Suburban was not reassuring.

"You guys start digging, I'll see if I can scout up some branches to stick under the wheels."

First light was now on us, and as I left, Dan, a plumber by trade and no stranger to the shovel, was already digging in front. The tamaracks we had seen a few miles back were the likeliest place for wood, so I headed back there. The desert is a tough place to find any kind of wood, so we'd have to use whatever I found. We weren't in a position to be choosy. Within an hour I was back with a good load of wood and branches. Dan had the front wheels exposed, but Paul had not brought a jack along. This was not only going to be tough, it was going to be next to impossible without a jack. Dan and I tried lifting the front end and managed a centimeter or two. With Paul's help, we got her up a bit more, then miraculously wedged branches and wood under both wheels. We checked the back tires and they still seemed okay, but there was no question there was unseen water below them. Paul got in and Dan and I pushed, first backward then forward, a rocking motion that gradually got the Suburban moving to and fro. Finally, we nudged her, then she climbed up on the mud and moved forward to dry ground. There was a small celebration, plenty of self-congratulations around, and a victory photo. Then we got down to the business of getting back on the road, for although we were now unstuck, it appeared we were on a small island, surrounded by impassable sink mud. We gathered more branches and limbs, and then marked out which path would be least damp. Paul goosed it, and got three feet before the front end nosed in. *Now* we were stuck – really stuck.

Paul and Dan surveyed the situation, loaded up guns and dekes and headed off towards the ponds.

"Hey you guys, we're not going to just leave it here, are we?"

"No, but nobody else is going to take it either, so we might as well hunt."

"I'll tell you what. Over those sand dunes about five or ten miles is Luis B. Encinas. I'll hike over there and see if we can get any sympathy . . . or help."

"Suit yourself," said Paul, as he and Dan disappeared into the swamps.

First light had come and gone, and a peculiar sky had now developed; there was dark grey above us, blue to the north, and *lots* of wind. Although I couldn't make it out, I knew approximately where the water tower marking Luis

B. Encinas was, and figured I would be able to spot it if I climbed the nearest sand dune, a couple miles off. By the time I got near the dunes, the wind had kicked up so bad that it was hard to walk into it. Literally, it seemed to be forcing me backwards; that and the sand that was stinging my face and hands made this a rather unpleasant task. Occasionally I looked back towards the ponds and could see ducks working. The boys would be having a fine shoot. Cresting the dunes, I got my first glance of Luis Encinas. It looked like my estimate of five to ten miles was a bit conservative, and it had taken an hour to go this far. I started wishing I had brought some water, but what the heck; no point in going back now. Going down the other side was slower going still, as now the wind really picked up. From the intensity of it, I guessed we were in the land portion of a Sea of Cortez *chubasco*. I laid down in the sand, covered my face, and decided to ride it out.

Forty five minutes later, it was still blowing, but the bulk of the storm was now further north. I plugged on, and two hours later walked into Luis B. Encinas. On a good day there might be one vehicle in town. Today was exceptional in that there were two. The closest was a shiny white new Chevy pick-up, with the bedecked owner proudly leaning up against the fender, and, he was dressed in a coat and bolo tie, no less. Obviously this was some *patron* down here checking on his farming operation. He proved to be a good listener, then to my relief said, of course, he would help.

We drove back out to the swamps by a back route, and he surveyed the situation. He had a long rope which he secured to the Suburban, then with me at the wheel, he tried to yank it out. After several tries, it was apparent his truck just couldn't get the traction needed, and another plan was in order. We discussed several possibilities, but it was obvious we would need a big winch and an A-frame to get this beauty out. He asked if we'd need a ride into Coahuila for lodging, and I said yes, but if he could return at dark, it would be better. He thought this odd, but it was useless to try and explain it to him. I wouldn't be able to get Paul and Dan out of the swamps 'til dark. So off he went, with plans to secure an A-frame tow truck in the morning, and us later that night.

I didn't feel much like hunting, but wandered off into the swamps to find the boys. They had changed positions from when I had earlier seen them from atop the sand dunes. Now they were farther into the swamp, and still shooting up a storm. I found them within an hour and laid out the plans, but they were much more concerned with how much ammunition I had brought with me; they were both low.

We shot the rest of the afternoon, then headed in before dark to be sure and catch our ride back to town. Guillermo was there waiting for us, and after loading up guns and ducks, we headed for Estación Coahuila.

There's not much to Coahuila, and services of any kind are spotty. So, it was no real surprise when Guillermo informed us there was no tow truck . . . unless, that is, we could get hold of a CB radio and get one that way. He thought on that for a few miles, then said simply, "*Policiá.*"

Hey, there was an idea! Three unshaven *gringos*, full of mud, cold, tired, wet, hungry, and going to the police station. Actually, this was the *one* place in Coahuila I'd never been to – on purpose. Guillermo, or Willy, as he said to call him, parked in front of the police station, and the two of us went in. The police were both understanding and gracious, and gave us full use of their CB. Speaking Spanish is one thing; listening to a bunch of Mexican tow truck drivers all on the same channel is another. Finally, Willy thought that one guy over at Kilometer 43 understood our needs, and agreed to meet us at eight next morning.

We had been inside quite some time and were unprepared for what awaited us in the truck. Somehow Dan or Paul had come up with a bottle of Jack Daniels, and between them had polished it off. Both were asleep in the truck cab, along with Snowflake. Some of the whiskey had been spilled in the cab and it reeked of alcohol. As we opened the doors, Dan looked up, stuck his head outside, and vomited all over the police parking area; and not just once, but twice for good measure.

I put Paul and the dog in back, and then Willy drove us to the "hotel."

"Willy, I don't recall seeing a hotel in Coahuila."

"Oh, *sí señor*. Has been here very long time."

We drove straight into the center of town, and just off the main drag, pulled up next to the town's largest and most impressive structure, the church. Willy led the way around back and we met some drunk who extracted $1.75 from me for two rooms. There was one bed per room, but we could share, he said. With the carnival in town accommodations were hard to come by. We unloaded Paul, the guns and dog, thanked Willy profusely, and planned to meet here in the morning.

The "hotel" was adobe and built onto the church as an afterthought. The carnival was jammed up against the church also, complete with typical blaring loud speakers, overly loud music, and zillions of people. Actually, I'd never seen a carnival down here, so this was kind of interesting. We checked out the rooms, and Paul and his lab crashed in one bed. Dan looked skeptically at our room before entering. The ceiling was earthen, and there were two one-by-four boards, 15 feet each, criss-crossed in the center, and suspiciously looking like they were holding up the sagging ceiling. Dan entered, full of mud and soaking wet, laid in the bed and instantly rolled towards the middle. Ah ha! This wasn't a bed, it was a hammock. It would be cute sleeping with him in that. Paul and the dog, meanwhile, were already asleep.

The thought of sleep was alluring, but the damn carnival was so noisy that I decided on dinner instead. I walked back out and gingerly stepped over the human excrement in the "courtyard" in front of our rooms. There evidently was no outhouse, so if you had the urge, you just let 'er fly, and the management came around with a shovel next day. Outside it was a whole lot more pleasant than in those two rooms, so I hit the *carnicería* and *panadería* for meat and bread before stopping for a quart of Tecate at the ice house. The rain that day had cut the dust, so now Coahuila was one big mud bog instead of the usual dust bowl.

Estación Coahuila, now there's a place. The *"Estación"* part was because the train from Mexicali south stopped here, prior to the long run down to Mexico City. *"Coahuila"* – I don't know where that came from, but it represented every kind of hardship and hope one could imagine.

For a town of some ten to twenty thousand, it had an adequate police force. Running water that was safe to drink, however, was another matter. There was always enough bread at the *panadería* and fresh *tortillas* at the *tortilleria*, but most of the *indios* could not afford to buy even the cheapest cuts of beef or chicken. Pork, also, was unaffordably high. As for beans, they had stayed relatively affordable, although they had doubled in cost relative to the pay scales. Rice . . . forget it; available but way too expensive. *Verduras*, or vegetables, could be found in the two markets, but again, most food money went to beans.

The ice house is part of the culture, because this town is like many in the U.S. in the late 1800's to early 1900's – no refrigeration, except for the very well-to-do. Most food stores have refrigeration, but fully 99% of the homes do not. Hence, trips to the ice house are mandatory if one needs to keep foods cool. Additionally, the ice house serves as the Tecate distributorship, so most cold beer is also purchased there.

If you are sick or have an accident, the local doctor's office is available six days per week. It is not more than a couple of poorly lit rooms, with capabilities for simple x-rays. Never having been in to see the local docs, it is difficult to comment on their level of expertise.

The local car wash is at the far end of town, but most

folks usually use the Colorado river for their car wash; also it makes a good family outing. Local vendors of clothes, hardware, shoes, food, tires, auto parts, beer and liquor are all are found next to one another on the main drag. The church and whorehouses are off on side streets. There is always a throng of people milling around town. People of all ages, some well-dressed, some barefoot, can be seen working, browsing, or just conversing with a neighbor. It is a friendly town, where, if a stranger has a problem, the local citizenry is likely to help. Coahuila is certainly not a destination seen on any travel brochures, but it is a friendly place, with good, hard-working people. There are no beggars, as the prevailing attitude is if you need money, work for it. Last, but not least, are the three or four Pemex stations at which you can get gasoline, but gas in small towns in Mexico is notorious for having water in it. An in-line water filter for the fuel pump is not a bad idea if one travels much down here. But the overall feeling of Coahuila, if one were to ask, for me, would be dust. Twelve months a year dust hangs in the air in town, unless it is immediately after a rain.

And so it was this evening, everything all mudded up following the afternoon's rain. Walking through town in the mud was actually kind of pleasant in a way, because now you didn't have to breathe the infernal dust. Somewhat later I returned to our room and fell instantly asleep.

Dan kept rolling on me all night because of the bed, but even at that it was better than being in the desert with no food, no blankets, no *nada*. Our wake-up call came at six a.m., when the church bells gonged us awake. Wow, they were loud. Our entire room vibrated with each clang, and dirt from the ceiling fell in spite of the 1x4's. None of us could withstand the racket, so we piled out, found the first working taco stand, and then proceeded to eat all the proprietor could cook. Once again, the proximity of the ice house meant beer, not coffee, for breakfast.

We waited an hour for eight o'clock to come around; then at nine, waited for ten. Finally, at eleven Willy appeared, leading a beaten-up old tow truck with A-frame and winch to pick us up. We piled in and headed back towards the swamps. By the time we got there, however, there were at least forty or more people looking at the half buried Suburban. It was something new, and was cheap entertainment for all the folks from Luis B. Encinas. They had heard of the predicament yesterday, and were here today to watch the fun.

The first attempt was a simple hook-up of the tow truck's winch to the Suburban's frame. The winch took up slack and pulled the Suburban slightly forward, then began to bend the frame out of shape. Basically, they were winching us sideways instead of straight ahead. Paul mentioned that to the tow truck owner, and he agreed straight ahead would be better. So he repositioned his rig, but had to be in some dicey areas to do so. We hooked up again and he winched up forward a bit before his winch motor overheated, then froze up. The smoke from the winch was a dead giveaway that the motor was toast. We needed a new plan.

"Just have him pull us out," said Paul.

I translated this to the driver, and he nodded. He put her in low gear and revved her up. Great! One foot, two feet, then a spinning of the truck tires and we watched, horrified, as the tow trunk sank into the slop. He must have been on a thin crust, and with the added weight, had just punched through. Now, not only were we stuck, but the tow truck was, too. Guillermo volunteered his Chevy to act as weight against which to winch. The only problem was that the tow winch was torched, so we had to have Willy pull the tow truck forward with his rope. He got a little traction on the first try; on the second, he sank into the earth in the middle of the desert. Obviously, there had been water under him also. I had always had a grudging respect for this place, but it was much more treacherous than I had realized. Dan slogged out to the Suburban, took out the shovel, and in forty five minutes, dug the front wheels free. Then we attached our winch to the A-frame, put her in four wheel drive and winched and four-wheeled out of the slop. There was a general murmuring approval from the gathered onlookers. Paul had Dan move over and put her in gear and off we went, much to my amazement and the utter shock of our would be rescuers.

"Paul, what about those guys?" I asked.

"Ah, screw 'em. Let's go hunting."

"Palmer, you *can't* do that. I know many of those people back there. If we did that, next time down here, they'd skin me... and that's no exaggeration."

"Hey, they're inventive. They'll figure it out."

I reached over to grab the keys and turn off the ignition. Paul realized how serious I was, and capitulated. He turned her around, and headed us back to the two stuck trucks.

Guillermo was first to come over. "Ha, ha. You were just trying to trick us into thinking you would just leave us here. Ha, ha. That is a good joke *señor* . . ."

But I could tell by the quavering in his voice he might be a touch mad also. We winched Willy, then the tow truck out, paid them each for their helpfulness, and headed back towards our pheasant field. We shot a few more birds, but basically were happy to be heading home. I knew there'd be other days . . and there were.

Pez Gallo

Fumbling in the dark, I tried to find the irritating phone. "Hello."

"Stanton, this is Palmer. Meet at the Pez Gallo at four a.m."

"Paul, what time is it?"

"One a.m. There's a hot bite off the Coronados, and we have to be underway by four." Click.

I reached for the alarm and set it, then mercifully fell back asleep. Three hours later I joined Paul at the dock and we were gone. He had already gassed up, had live anchovies in the bait tank, and had all four rods rigged for a different eventuality. The Coronado Islands are some twelve miles off the Mexican coast, but are about 21 miles from San Diego on a south-southwest heading.

We were there before dawn, but good news travels fast on the water, and so there were a ton of other boats. We trolled feathers and jigs at first light, chummed anchovies every now and then, but didn't get into them. It was a beautiful day and watching the sunrise over these uninhabited islands was spectacular. Occasionally we'd see a sport fisher like us hook-up, but it always seemed to be just for one fish. Nobody seemed to be able to keep the school of yellowtail at their boat. There were also a few party boats out, slick looking jobs with fifteen to twenty fisherman on board.

"How about we make a pass real close to the island?"

"Okay with me, Paul. You're the boss."

For the next several hours we just trolled back and forth, up and back, in close, out far, but no strikes. Whenever Paul spotted a hook up, we'd speed over there, and troll around the boat with a fish on; but nothing, Paul knew they were here; he could feel it. As for me, the only thing I could feel was incipient sea sickness. It was always with me out on the ocean.

Around ten we spotted a couple of boils, a churning of water by big fish feeding on little ones. We trolled around, then through the boils, but always with the same result . . . nothing.

Paul had been staring at the new Frank LoPrieste boat, the *New Lo Ann*, and slowly turned us on a heading to coincide with its position. As we got close, I saw it too; there were at least eight or nine hook ups off the stern, and there was a continuous boil back there. The deck hands were throwing copious numbers of anchovies into the water, to keep the yellowtail congregated in that spot. As we came to within a quarter mile, it was obvious *everybody* was hooked up, and the yellowtail boil was really apparent now. As long as they kept fish on and continued chumming anchovies, the yellowtail would stay right there. Paul eased us in closer, and suddenly flicked a jig right into the middle of the boil.

"Hey, get the hell out of here!" yelled a fisherman from above.

Paul disregarded him and cast again into the boil. At very best we were no more than thirty feet behind their boat. There was a good chance he could foul hook somebody's fish or worse, scare the boil away. Still, Paul kept casting into the middle of the feeding frenzy.

"Paul, don't you think we oughta' back off a little?" I asked.

"Look, this is a free ocean and . . " Paul was interrupted by a bullhorn from above.

"You in the boat down there. This is the captain of the New Lo Ann. Get your God damned boat away from our boil."

Paul shot him the finger and once again cast near their stern. The captain jerked a rod away from the nearest man, reeled in the lead jig, and flung it down at our boat. The two pound jig with treble hook on the end bounced off our windshield with a resounding crack. Paul reeled in and threw his jig hard against the stern of the New Lo Ann, resulting in a resounding *thunk*.

That was all it took. Every man on board who wasn't hooked up, reeled in and started slinging his steel jig down at us. The windshield cracked, then cracks and dings in the fiberglass appeared in concert with the unending barrage of *thunk, crack, crack, thud, thud, crack, thunk*. Not only were they slinging those 2 lb. lead jigs down at us, but with those ugly treble hooks on the end, they were trying to *snag-hook* us.

Paul got the message, and we backed out of treble hook-jig range. He still teased them with a few casts into the boil, but sensing the futility of the situation, we moved on. There were numerous other strikes that day, but wouldn't you know it, we got none. Probably it was what we deserved.

There was some talk on the way in about trying again next day, but after today's fiasco, I was content to let it ride. We talked about the upcoming hunting season in Baja, and how we'd better start thinking about applying for hunting licenses. I was just not interested in fishing anymore for awhile. Paul agreed, but I knew he'd be back out there tomorrow, whether I joined him or not.

A week passed and since I hadn't heard from Paul by Saturday night, I figured I was safe for another week. The phone rang just past midnight.

"Hot yellowtail bite off La Jolla cove. Meet at the dock at 4 a.m." Click.

This time I didn't even get a word in before he hung up.

Four a.m. sharp we met at the dock, but this time the other co-owners of the boat were there, too. Between us only Paul and Schultze had caught yellowtail before. Leo, Strumpford, and I had yet to connect. For me, it was two and a half years and still no yellowtail; some of it had been bad luck, but some of it was just plain bad technique. Paul was going to do his darndest to catch us some fish. Expectantly, we shoved off a little after four- fifteen.

The trip up the coast was rough, and took longer than expected, so it wasn't until first light that we actually arrived off the cove. And what a sight. Dunkirk could not possibly have looked much different from this. As far as the eye could see, there were boats – thousands and thousands of them. We tried to guesstimate just how many, and arrived at the figure of somewhere between five and ten thousand. Not only that, but they were packed in like sardines. At no place could you see where two boats were any more than twenty yards apart. This meant that as far as the eye could see, in all directions, it was just *solid* boats. The amazing thing was, it looked like they all had hook-ups.

The five of us got to the task of getting baited up and getting in the water, but as usual, Paul was first in. He got a strike almost immediately, but was a fraction slow and missed it. From the stern, bow, amidships, we proceeded to cast our arms off; squid, anchovies, jigs, feathers, more anchovies, more squid, more anchovies, and all the time, Paul was constantly chumming with anchovies – a few out the front, a few out the back, close in, way out, but *nothing* happened. It was incredible; moreover, it was unbelievably frustrating. Paul had also brought his new Visla puppy, Tsar, along, as he had chewed up a five thousand dollar sofa the previous evening, and couldn't be trusted alone in the house. Somebody mentioned putting a hook through him and tossing him overboard, but Paul would not hear of that. Finally, in utter desperation, Paul reached under the bow locker, pulled out his mask and snorkel, and proceeded to strip bare-assed naked in front of God and fifteen thousand people. In a flash he was overboard in the clear blue water that had recently moved in, bringing all the yellowtail. He swam around the boat then suddenly broke the surface and yelled, "Stanton, bait up a squid and be ready in the bow. Leo, bait up an anchovy and be ready in the stern. Be ready to cast exactly where I tell you."

With that, he was down again, and we watched the iridescent orange of his snorkel top, making circles around our boat. Suddenly, up he came and pointed 15 yards off the port bow. I was there in a second, and no sooner had that squid hit the water, than a boil of yellowtail erupted around it, slashing and hacking at the bait. *Bingo!* I was hooked up. I let 'em take it one, two, three seconds and gave a yank. Wow, what a fish! He swam straight away, then down, then charged the boat. Then he was down again. No wonder yellowtail are so highly sought after as a game fish.

Paul suddenly was up again, pointed astern, and Leo was there. Wham! Another hook-up, and we were jazzed. It took fifteen minutes to get my fish aboard, and when it finally happened, I thought back to those dozens of other dry runs I had made for this elusive fighter. It had been worth the wait.

No sooner was my fish boated than Paul was up again, pointing, and Schultze put it right on the mark and another hook-up. Every once in a while Paul's snow white buttocks would stick up above the water, bringing some odd looks, smiles, and indignant shouts from the dozen boats almost on top of us. A couple guys even started using Paul's spots as a guide, which really hacked him off. Considering last weekend, it occurred to me that Paul had either a short memory – or more likely, a rather pronounced double standard when it came to butting in on someone else's fishing spot.

Paul climbed up on the stern drive unit, and with quivering purple lips, handed me the mask and snorkel. I had my fish, now I was going to see what Paul had seen while in the water. Without a wetsuit, not to mention *any* suit, the water was *cold*. My teeth started to chatter the minute I got in, but darn, it was like looking into an aquarium. Fish were everywhere, and these babies were big. Yellowtail swim in schools, and to watch them glide effortlessly in no particular direction, then sense a bait, and violently attack it in a ferocious, slashing manner is an all time thrill. Any bait fish in their paths simply did not have a chance. I popped up half a dozen times, and each resulted in an instantaneous hook-up. Man, was this fun. Watching a feeding frenzy at eye level has to rate right up there with some of the most fascinating things I have ever seen. I didn't want to get out, but hypothermia was coming on, as I was having trouble moving my legs and arms, and my teeth chattered so loudly that it was hard to think.

Leo was next in as he had already boated two fish. In fact, everybody had two except Strumpford, and he still had zip. His first yellowtail was still in the ocean. Finally, it was Paul's turn again, and he was intent on getting Strumpford hooked-up if it took all day. In his first several strikes, it appeared Bob had reacted too quickly, and literally jerked the bait out of the attacker's mouth.

"Not so fast this time Bob. Let 'em take one, two, three seconds, then hammer 'em." With that, Paul was gone. Sure enough, less than a minute later he had Strumpford hooked-up, but after 25 minutes of fighting his fish, Paul got back in the boat, retrieved something, and was back in. Everyone was watching Strumpford, so we had barely noticed Paul. The next thing I recall is Bob's impassioned pleas, "No Paul, no. No!"

Palmer had been swimming in the general direction of Bob's fish, a good sized one, and had his speargun. He was going to shoot Bob's fish. "Paul, you dirty bounder. NO! Don't!"

With that, Paul pulled the trigger and in fascination and horror, we all watched as the spear streaked right at the fish, only to miss it by a fraction, as the fish turned hard left trying to shake the hook. He had missed, and the spear, which was not attached to the gun, disappeared into the blue water. Chagrined, Paul swam to the stern, got up on the stern drive unit and came in for the last time. Meantime, Strumpford had landed his fish amidst a chorus of "finally" and "well done."

Tsar, who had been a good dog to this point by not chewing up our upholstered seats – he did chew on the anchor rope a bit – began barking, and got his forepaws down on the stern drive unit, which was just at waterline. He barked several more times before Paul noticed and went to retrieve him; suddenly Paul lurched for Tsar just as a fourteen foot blue shark chomped down on the stern drive unit and propeller – just where Tsar had been plucked from. Being cheated of his dinner, he became enraged, circled once, and came back to ram and chomp on the stern drive and propeller again. None of us had ever seen anything like this before, and in horror we watched as this brute kept chomping on our propeller. Paul fired up the engine, and once in gear, the shark became more frenzied. He repeatedly attacked the spinning propeller and we couldn't believe it as teeth, mouth parts, and his upper and lower jaw fixed on those spinning blades. They say sharks feel no pain, but this was awesome. Shark mouth parts and blood were everywhere. Suddenly we were surrounded by sharks, and they began feasting on this crazed bleeding beast behind us. Soon it was all over in a swirling finale with sharks rolling, slashing, and ultimately completely devouring our intruder. Naturally, when sharks show up, the bite cuts off. And so it was; as constant and frantic a bite as it had been all day, it was now over. The sharks had broken up the yellowtails' feeding; there would be no more fish caught here today.

As hundreds, then thousands of boats packed it in and headed home, the long trail of fishermen headed back to Point Loma. Paul was elated, as not only had we all caught fish – good fish – but three of us finally had caught our

116

first yellowtail. For Paul it was a time for celebrating. The mood of the rest of us, though, was somewhat subdued. True, we had been part of a bite that some fishermen only dream about, yet never see. Additionally, we had seen the most magnificent spectacle under water, watching the yellowtail in a feeding frenzy.

But the shark had put a chill into all of us, for he had not been after Tsar. Rather, he had to have been watching those white skinned snorkelers, of which Paul was the last, and having been denied his feast, followed Paul right up to the stern drive when he finally got out. Why he didn't attack Paul, I have no idea. It was obvious from his attack on the boat just exactly what his intentions were. I think he was mad that he let Paul climb out of the water, instead of striking him sooner. Whatever, it had been a close call, and it could have just as well have been another of us earlier on. Paul was unconcerned because we got our fish and everything worked out all right.

I have thought about that day many times since then. We had a close call – a very close call. The stupidity of it hit me later. Of the five doctors on board, we must have had a combined IQ of about sixty for pulling a stunt like that. But it wouldn't be the last time – not by a long shot.

This was the same Palmer who called and said there were albacore on a 270° heading off Point Loma, 70 miles out.

"In our boat, Paul? Geez, the Pez Gallo is only 23 feet long. And we just have one engine."

Naturally, I went anyway, and six hours after leaving, the motor conked out, we had no water, and the radio didn't work. Six hours later, as we were drifting towards Japan, a freighter radioed our position to the Coast Guard.

Ah, the Coast Guard – they knew us well, having had to raise our boat from the bottom of the bay twice, after we launched it with no plug in. Of course, once steering cables, engine and whatever else is immersed in salt water, it never works as advertised again. Such was the case with the Pez Gallo. An interesting name that – the Pez Gallo. It translates from the Spanish as rooster fish, one of the most sought after, highly prized fighting fish in the Sea of Cortez. For that matter, on a pound for pound basis, I would put that fish up against any when it came to fighting fish. The Pez Gallo, on the other hand, was a joke. Being to the bottom twice, of course, did not help. But with multiple users, none of whom were interested in giving the time and care a boat demands – well, the Pez Gallo gave us pretty much what we deserved.

Paul was not interested in the boat per se. He was only interested in what it could do for us. Same went for fishing tackle. Paul had the world's best, but it never was in really top notch shape, because he never took the time to care for it. But if there was a new wrinkle, or a new fishing idea, Paul tried it first. Take the Colorado River fishing trip, for example.

We put in at Lee's Ferry, then motored upstream twelve miles just below Glen Canyon dam. First thing he and Hank did after taking out their rods, was to start taking apart ballpoint pens. Fascinated, I watched as they took the cartridges out, placed the hole end over the barbed hook with the writing portion of the cartridge pointing down. Next, out came the night crawlers, which were then threaded over the pen point, up the cartridge, over the hook and onto the line, until the end of the worm was advanced to the tip of the hook.

"You're kidding," I laughed.

Within a mile of drift they had each landed two rainbows in the five to eight pound range. I'd never dreamt there were trout like that. But leave it to Paul. *He knew.*

On that same trip, the goose season was open so we deked out a sand bar and watched as the honkers came on it. As we raised up to fire, the geese went straight up. One was crippled, but landed so far down the river, that by the time we got in the boat, he was gone. No problem. Paul had me climb the cliff about a hundred yards behind the dekes. I went up a hundred or so feet, with the river and

Paul below. Hank took the boat and went a mile down-stream. The next flight that came in, went straight up when Paul shot; for me they were eye level and I dropped two. Hank, a mile downstream, picked up the two dead geese. Only Palmer would have come up with that idea.

On and on it went; new ideas, new spots, new tech-niques – Paul knew 'em all and made them work. On one trip, Paul, my dad and I were out for yellowtail, and in big rolling seas Paul says, "See that kelp pad about half a mile ahead? Well there's a giant sunfish under it and directly under that there's at least a twenty pound yellowtail."

"C'mon Palmer. What kelp pad?"

"There, see it?"

Dad and I saw it several minutes later, and as we came near, spotted the huge sunfish underneath. Incredibly, below him was a huge yellowtail.

"C'mon you guys, be ready. Get some good casts down there."

Anytime after that when I talked to my dad about Paul, he always said, "You mean *x-ray* eyes?" He did have good eyes. But the thing was, Paul *knew* that fish was there. It was uncanny – which brings us to the halibut trip.

The San Diego Union had been running stories on the huge halibut being taken off the Tijuana bull ring, just eight to ten miles south of San Diego. The intrepid five showed up at times ranging between five and seven a.m., much to Paul's dismay, and finally we were off. Just as I cast the line off the Pez Gallo, Paul announced that there was a big fish roast on the beach tonight at the La Jolla Beach and Tennis Club, and he had invited seventy some couples. "So boys, we better catch some fish."

Well, you had to admire his confidence in our abilities, but nonetheless, it seemed kind of risky to assume we'd boat enough halibut to feed 150 people.

We no sooner were off the bull ring than Schultze hooked-up, then Strumpford, then Paul. Three hook-ups all at once. Wow, that's fishing! Leo finally snagged one, but we fished all day, and I didn't get a tap. Hey, some days are like that. I was just snakebit, that's all. But the rest of the boys, they caught fish.

Early afternoon we called it quits, and headed in. Schultze had offered his place to clean these beauties, which was going to be a chore, as we had darn near 300 pounds of halibut. Schultze had an actual fish cleaning room in his house; no surprise when you learn that his magnificent old home used to be a hunting and fishing lodge in San Diego around the turn of the century. It was magnificent, and afforded us a great place to steak out all these halibut. Although everyone was a physician, not all were eager to get their hands dirty. To me, it was no big deal; fish blood, duck blood, it was all the same.

I had no sooner cut the first two steaks, when I thought I saw something move in the intestines. Egad! This behemoth was filled with worms. Well, that was no problem. We had tons of fish so I just set this one aside. I called Paul's attention to this discovery and he just shrugged his shoulders. Next one was the same; in fact all the guys spotted worms in the intestines. Paul assured us it was no sweat; we weren't eating the guts. But when I steaked the meat, each and every piece was full of worms; hundreds of them were in each and every piece. We had a hundred and fifty people counting on us for fish steaks, and all we had was three hundred pounds of worm-infested halibut.

"Paul, this is *no bueno*. We can't use these steaks – heck, there's more worms than halibut in most of 'em."

"Nah, it's okay. We'll just cook 'em real well; and besides, the party's at night. Nobody's going to see what he's eating."

I tried a few more times, but Paul just wouldn't hear of it. Of course, the reason all these halibut had worms was because they are bottom feeders, and feeding off the Tijuana and bull ring sewage, they just couldn't help but get worms.

We didn't finish cleaning fish until late and by then it

was time to head for La Jolla Beach and Tennis Club. When we arrived, the fires were already going, the potato salad, bread, vegies and drinks were in place; everyone was delighted to see us and they ooohed and ahhed over the fish. We cooked it up – *well* – and with everything else, sat down to a truly scrumptious spread. When the fish platter came around to me, though, I quickly passed it on. "What's the matter, Stanton? Have some halibut. Hell, you caught it."

"Yeah, I did. Just not much of fish eater," I said. But my thoughts were, "Just not *this* fish."

El Diá de Gracias

'll tell you what, Alan. You come out here and we'll show you the finest duck hunt you've ever dreamed of, your duck lease in those rice ponds west of Houston notwithstanding."

And so I was a bit chagrined as we drove up not only to the now dry channel through which we had pulled our boat, but later we drove right up to Duarte pond itself; or rather *into* the pond. Now Duarte is usually two miles across and three to four miles long; today it was just a shrunken up mud hole no more than 300 yards across in any direction. This was a joke. How in the world were we going to hunt a two inch deep mud hole with nary a twig for cover?

We drove to a place on the pond's south side, where I had deked out many times over the years; now we set up a tent there. A blue norther had blown in and the temperature had dropped into the low 40's, with a cloudless blue sky. That fantastic hunt I had promised Alan was starting to look a bit oversold. Okay. A *lot* oversold. But he took it all in good stride. I hadn't seen my old roommate since college days at University of Texas. Jimmy, his twin brother and I had ended up living only a mile from one another in San Clemente, near Nixon's western white house. Together we had planned this trip, but it had been like pulling teeth to finally get Alan out here. Actually, the three of us went back to high school days when Alan, Jim, their neighbor Steve, and I had played basketball, two on two each night after basketball practice. In addition to that, Ian and Jean Stewart had become my favorite "other parents." Later, in medical school years, we all played bridge, drank Shandigaffs and generally had great fun together. To have Alan out now was tremendous, but I felt a little stupid with the mud hole in front of our tent.

While we reminisced about old times, I was desperately trying to come up with a game plan for tomorrow's hunt. The day itself was taken care of; we would cook a turkey in a buried bed of coals all day, and then celebrate El Diá de Gracias – Thanksgiving – with homemade pumpkin pie and whipped cream. My daughters and their mom were in charge of eats, which would be splendid. As the hours rolled by, the plans for the hunt began to look really grim. While they all chatted, I hiked back out to the middle of the mud hole for some inspiration. Cover was the big thing; there was none. And anything we brought out there would stick out like a sore thumb and flare the birds away. So, we had to think low profile. Low profile. That's it! Low profile. We'd take some plywood out to the pond, sink it into the water at a 15° angle, so the shooter could have his head and shoulders slightly elevated out of the water. Then you would suck up your guts and lay down on the board, with only the gun, head and shoulders slightly out of the water. Sounded good, so I headed in, took out my plywood sheets (used for traction when stuck in the mud), and cut them up into three 8 foot pieces. Jim and Alan noticed me cutting the plywood with the axe, but didn't really comment on it. Then with a rope handle on each board, the sled also served as a decoy bag carrier.

I couldn't decide whether to tell Alan and Jim the plans or not, because that water was plenty cold and I didn't want them thinking about it all night. We built a huge bonfire that night in our cooking pit, which burned down to beautiful cooking coals next morning at four a.m. The boys were rousted out and we had coffee while we dressed by the fire.

"How we gonna play this?" asked Alan.

When I explained, I got some mighty incredulous looks, but these guys figured I knew what I was doing.

"You mean lie down *in the water*? Jesus, man, it be cold!"

Well, I couldn't argue much with Alan's conclusion, but it was the best we had.

"No waders, huh?"

"Nope. This norther blew in on our way down here. Last week it was in the 80's when we hunted doves up near the border."

First light was 45 minutes off, so we headed out to set the dekes, then to get ourselves set. With six dozen decoys on that small body of water, any self-respecting duck would have to decoy in. But we had to stay low. As we eased into the water, the coldness stung our skin. Alan and Jim were two inches taller than I at 6'3", so we had to get them deeper yet. Finally, 30 minutes before first light we were set. Our three boards were huddled fairly close together, so when Jimmy's teeth began to chatter, Alan and I both heard it. "Ga-ga-ga-God, it's cold," was all Jim could get out. "Muh, muh-muh-my hands are so cold, I ca-ca-ca-can't fa-fa-fa-feel my fingers. I think I've ga-ga-ga-gotta go in."

"Jeez, Jim. Just a few more minutes."

"Fa-fa-fa-fa-few more minutes, fa-fa-fa-fooey. I'll be dea-dea-dea-dead by then."

"Okay, I'll give you a hand. Al, hold my gun. C'mon Jimbo."

He was like a solid block of ice. He had gotten so cold that neither his feet, arms nor legs worked. I rubbed him down a bit, got him going in the direction of the tent, then got back into the water.

"Larry, the only reason this water isn't frozen is because it's salty. I guarantee it would be frozen if it weren't for the sa-sa-sa-sa-salt."

Oh boy, now it was Alan's turn.

"What do you think, Al? Can you make it another 10 minutes? Be first light then."

"Shu-shu-shu-shu-sure."

And then in the starlight I watched as his hands went into spasm.

"Holy cats. I'm duh-duh-duh-done."

So I helped Al out of the mud and water, headed him into camp, and then slogged back into the icy water. He was not quite at the campfire when first light broke through the low cloud layer, attended by the cold wind that usually comes at dawn. Man was it cold! I probably hadn't frozen up yet because I'd been out of the water twice getting the boys back to camp. But I could feel it now. This half-baked idea had to make the all time stupid list. On top of which, there weren't going to be any – uh oh - ducks. Could that be on the horizon... It was! Headed straight in, came a triplet, moving low and fast, right to the dekes. The lead bird passed four inches over my head – never saw me – and as the pair came in, I raised up in ice-slow-motion, and pulled on 'em. "Boom! Ba-woom!" The echo shook the wonderful stillness, which was followed by a "splash, splash." Two. Got the pair. They weren't going anywhere, but it was so dang cold, I needed to get up to get the blood circulating. I had been cold before, but this was the champ. My toes hurt, my fingers throbbed, my skin burned from the fierce cold. Worst part was, nobody was holding me here. I was doing this to myself. I retrieved the pair, but was unable to identify them in the low light. I slid my fingers into their belly feathers for warmth, but that didn't help the painful pounding in my toes.

Fifteen minutes more, and I gave in to the inevitable. I let the dekes stay where they were; we could bag 'em up later. I just had to get out of this ice water. Only on the way in did I notice. Canvasbacks! I had never seen any before. These boys were way off their beaten flight path, as they normally migrate along the Atlantic flyway. They were occasionally seen in the central flyway, but never out here. When the birds were later mounted, Huey, the taxidermist, remarked that he hadn't known of any Cans taken in Baja since the 40's. Wow! What a surprise. This made the hunt worthwhile after all. But believe me, that was a hard sell with Jimmy and Alan. They were both dead to the world in their down mummy bags, with tons of blankets piled on top of each. The kids helped throw the tinfoiled turkey in the coals, and then we covered him up with Duarte pond silt. The cold ache in my bones hadn't gone away, so I bagged it also, waking in time for dinner. Jimmy and Alan stayed under wraps all day, but when the turkey was dug up that afternoon, the aroma brought them both out of their bags.

The Mexicans don't have a *diá de gracias*, but we had as fine a spread as anyone anywhere that Thanksgiving afternoon – slow roasted turkey in a pit, mashed potatoes, cranberry sauce, gravy and pumpkin pie with whipped cream we had brought down in the ice chest. As we sat around the campfire that night, I thought about all we had to be thankful for – good friends, good food, good health. The latter, however, was disproven several days later, when Alan came down with pneumonia upon returning to Houston.

Jimmy and I continued to see one another upon returning home; but Alan – Alan I didn't see again 'til four years later when I returned home to Houston to spend Thanksgiving with my folks. Alan lived on the other side of Houston, an hour and a half away, but I thought it would be nice to give him a call. It was just like old times, and he wanted to know if we could get together. My brother was coming over Saturday for a game of bridge, but Friday was open – if my mom would understand. She didn't, but when I told her Alan was going duck hunting in the morning and invited me, she softened up a little. That morning at 3 a.m. I was at Alan's, and off we headed.

"I don't need any gear?"

"Nah, I've got everything you need at the club."

When we arrived at the "club," there were already a dozen guys there drinking coffee laced with brandy, telling tales and getting dressed – *warmly* – for the morning's hunt. He introduced me around – they had heard about the Baja hunt – and then one of them said, "Stewart, why don't you take Section 8, over there near Chewy?"

"Sure."

As I looked around, I thought about the stark contrasts between this duck club and our duck hunts in Baja. Toilets, showers, kitchen, beds, automatic duck pickers – just like at home. In no way, shape, or form did this remind me of Mexico. It was just too civilized.

Alan began putting on his waders, down coat, down mittens, all of which went over his down underwear. He told me I'd be fine in my jeans, but would need a pair of waders, which he produced from the closet. Extra large, they looked like they would fit just right.

"Uh, Alan? There seems to be a rip here from the crotch to the knee."

"Really? Well, just wear 'em, and we'll stay out of deep water. It's not really that cold out."

Right. The first three steps we took into the pond were to break the ice. After that, it got worse. First, one foot up on the ice, then the other, then crunch, down through the ice you would go. Basically, the shins took the brunt of the beating from the ice. Also, if it started to get a little deeper, you really didn't know until you broke through the ice and by then it was too late. My holey waders had filled with ice water after five minutes, and my feet felt like blocks of ice. Then they started to throb and really hurt, just before they went numb. We kept going through the rice paddies until Alan motioned me over to the well-hidden blind. Made of wood, with two benches, it was camouflaged beautifully, and allowed the hunter to sit up rather than stoop over when the ducks were coming in. Unfortunately, by the time we got situated on the stools, my feet were throbbing with pain. First light came and nothing. Then the clouds lifted and there were the ducks – at 10,000 feet and moving south.

"Nice day," said Alan.

"Yep. But we're gonna need anti-aircraft guns to bring those beauties down."

I put my gun down, cut off the waders, and tried warming my feet by rubbing them with my hands. Alan looked sympathetic, but I knew he was thinking about his immersion in ice water four years before on our Baja hunt.

"Hey, Al. Do pintail ever deke in when the decoys are frozen in the water like that?"

"Sure, All the time. We just need cloud cover, that's all."

He hadn't gotten the words out of his mouth when in came a single sprig, wings locked, feet down, and just before he hit the ice, "ba-woom," I dropped him. The darn thing slid another thirty yards on the ice, even though he was stone dead. I watched, amazed that the ducks would actually come into decoys set into ice.

"Nice shootin'."

"Had you been looking that direction, you would have had him too."

This was the berries. You didn't have to lie down in the water, the dekes were already out, a stool to sit on, everything except warm feet. I mean, my toes were hurtin'.

"Alan, I'm gonna have to go out and pick up that sprig."

"Nah, it's not going anywhere. Just leave it."

"Big Al, I know it's not going anywhere. I just have to move around to warm my feet up. They're killing me."

"Suit yourself. But that bird dropped over there near Chewy. He'll get it."

I looked over that way, but if there was a blind there, I sure didn't see it.

"Jeez, you know my feet are so cold I'm afraid they're gonna get frostbite. I guess these waders with the hole in 'em kinda evens us up for the Baja hunt, huh?"

"Yeah, well, almost."

"It was that bad, huh?"

"Hell, Stanton. It was so cold in that damn pond I wasn't worried about frostbite, I was worried about dying. I guess you know I ended up with double walking pneumonia when I got home; missed three weeks of work, and spent two weeks in bed."

"It can get pretty cold in Baja," I agreed.

"Yeah, especially when your buddy sticks you in water up to your neck, in freezing water. At least I gave you a pair of waders."

"With holes in them," I reminded him.

Enough talk. I had to get the circulation going in my feet so I got off the stool and headed out of the blind towards the downed bird. *Crack, crack, crunch, crunch,* went the ice as every step required first getting on top of it and then breaking through. The dead sprig was about 50 yards away, and it took a full 15 minutes to get half way there. I pressed on because the physical activity was helping immensely with restoring circulation and warmth to my toes. Suddenly from behind me, I thought I heard a crack in the ice. It was at a different angle from which I had come, but I paid it no mind until I heard a distinctive, *crack, crack, crack, crunch, crunch, crack....* almost as if someone were running on the ice. Turning slightly to the right I saw the noisemaker. To my horror, it was a 14 foot alligator, lean, mean and hungry, and he was making tracks for that sprig. It was incredible! I thought all cold blooded reptiles laid down and went to sleep for the winter. No one ever told me they were racing around frozen rice ponds retrieving ducks in mid-winter.

I took two more steps towards the sprig and the alligator, sensing my intent, really turned it on. He covered the next 50 yards in a heartbeat, swooped the bird up in his jaws, and clamped down with an audible *"crunch,"* then turned his head towards me with those huge gaping jaws. Man, I couldn't get out of there fast enough. I streaked

129

back through the broken ice in record time, covering the 30 yards in 30 seconds. The 'gator made a move towards me, but it probably was intended as a threat more than anything else.

Alan had set his gun down and was slapping his knees and holding his sides guffawing for all he was worth.

"I told you Chewy would pick it up. He doesn't like people messing with his birds."

"Stewart, you dirty bounder. You bastard! You shoulda told me!"

"Hey amigo. *Now* call us even."

Luis B. Encinas

Don't look now, Herb, but we've got a cop on our tail."
A quick glance in the side mirror told him it was
so. The Blazer was so packed in back that the rearview mirror was useless. We had been so engrossed
in the telling of hunting stories that both of us had been
unaware of our speed creeping up; also we were still elated that we had made it through L.A. on Highway 10, just
before the mud slides closed it completely. It rained so
hard back there we couldn't believe it. Then, when the
mountains of mud started sliding down, and closing off
the freeway, we thought our long-planned trip had had it.
But we were lucky; we were one of the very last vehicles to
get through. The jubilation spilled over into our conversation and thoughts, all the way down to Indio, where we
had picked up a highway patrolman's flashing red light.

"Damn," exhaled Herb, as he crushed the beer can,
kicked it under the seat and put four sticks of spearmint
gum in his mouth. He pulled over, gave the gum a real
good chewing, then hopped out of the Blazer and went
back to see the patrolman.

"Doin' over 75," I heard, followed by out-of-earshot
mumblings. Sneaking a look in the rearview mirror, I saw
Herb and the CHP guy shaking hands. There was some
laughter, Herb's billfold identification came out, and then
maybe another ten minutes chat, but never any hint of

writing up a ticket. Shortly after, Herb returned and the CHP guy drove off with a wave.

"That was close."

"Yeah, you silver-tongued fox. What'd you tell him?"

"Just that I was with Coastal Division, just transferred, and this was my first time off in nine months."

"Figured as much. Boy you sure got that gum in your mouth quick. Good thinkin'."

Herb smiled. But I kinda figured we had this ticket beaten from the git-go. *Herb* was a highway patrolman.

Our elation was dimmed slightly, but we regained it as we neared Mexicali and the border check. So far, we had just missed the mud slides, just missed a speeding ticket, and were ready to cross the border. That, folks, is a good day. I always get jitters going through Mexicali. If some idiot runs into you, you can end up going to jail – that is, of course, unless you have Mexican insurance. Still, there are the ever present *policia*, looking for any real or imagined infraction, ready to haul you off to jail unless you choose to pay a little *mordida*. Although initially I abhorred this system, now I kind of like it, because you can pay your fine on the spot and get on down the road, no worries. Naturally, this may lead to over-zealousness on the part of the police when it comes to writing tickets. But hey, no system's perfect. Once through the border, we headed for the huge *supermercado* in Mexicali. I wanted a hundred pounds of rice and two hundred of beans. Additionally we got six cases of Tecate, and ten pounds of coffee. Don Emilio and Mamacita would be happy to see us.

We left Mexicali city limits at dusk, and arrived at Lupe's after dark. Everybody was bedded down so Herb and I just said hello and crossed the canal to set up camp under the tamarack.

The first day of duck season was tomorrow and being a Wednesday, we didn't expect much competition. Since moving to central California up in the Paso Robles area, I had been down infrequently, and therefore, had had no time to do any scouting for ducks. Our plan was simple enough – take the boat down to the swamp, launch it and scout for any potential flyways. If we got in a shoot, better still. While sitting around the campfire enjoying dinner, Lupe came by and said there was a field down the road which was flooded, and ducks had been feeding in it. Boy, was that good news.

"How far down?"

"No mucho. Menos de un kilómetro."

"How about a Tecate, Lupe?"

"Sí, gracias."

"Muchos patos?" I asked.

"Sí."

"Grandes o pequeños ?"

"Todos."

"What'd he say? What'd he say?" questioned Herb.

"Could be really hot news. Less than a kilometer down the road, there's a flooded field with ducks feeding in it— both big and small ducks. You wanna go take a look?"

"Tonight?"

"Sure. We'll finish up dinner and then just drive down the road a piece, just to see what we're up against."

"Uhh ... okay. Why not?"

"What are we going to see in the dark?"

"Finish your dinner and you'll see."

An hour later we had pitched our tent, placed the beans inside for safe keeping, along with sleeping bags, and set the rest of camp up outside on some cooktables. Decoys, guns and ammo were all kept outside. The drive down the road was a short one indeed. The field being flooded happened to be the one we were camped next to. It ran probably two to three miles in length, but was maybe only a quarter of a mile in width. And it was wet... real wet. The roughly plowed rows had at least six to eight inches of water in them, and the whole field was a mud bog. Tonight was a dark moon, perfect for hunting, and the starlight actually allowed one to see not all that badly.

"Let's have a look."

"Out there?"

"Yeah. It's just mud." And out we went. Each step we sank in to above the knees, and walking in mud like that is no picnic.

"Listen. Hear that? Let's get down. Flat."

"Jeez, I don't know. That water's kinda cold and the air's chilly."

A bit more of a harangue, and Herb got down. Man! The ducks were *really* working this field. They sensed us down below, so they made pass after pass over us, before finally succumbing to that primeval urge to feed. And down they went. "*Whoosh, whosh, whoooosh, splash!*" Hundreds of ducks! And they just kept coming in. In half an hour we must have had a thousand birds land all around us.

"I've seen enough. Let's call it a night."

Herb was only too glad to oblige. We headed back for camp, took off the muddy stuff and hung it on branches near the fire.

As I was contemplating how we were going to hunt this field in the morning, Herb said, "God, I wish I had a Big Mac."

We would have made it through the mud slides with several hours to spare, earlier today, except for Herb's need to stop at every McDonald's or Kentucky Fried Chicken. Personally, I couldn't stomach the stuff, but during his years on the CHP, it was a ritual to stop at these fast food places ... often. And now he was doing a poor imitation of a Big Mac withdrawal.

"Forget it Herb, I'll take you into Zacatecas tomorrow." Boy, was he in for a surprise.

"You figured out how we're gonna hunt that field?"

"I got an idea."

I think Herb suspected the answer, so he didn't ask. We bagged it underneath the stars, and a quick five hours later it was five o'clock.

"Be light in forty-five minutes, Herb. Shake a leg."

I made coffee and *huevos rancheros* for breakfast, cleaned up the dishes, then loaded the dekes, waders, guns, ammo, and drove those down to the flooded portion of the field; when I got back, it was getting dangerously close to first light.

"Herb, we've got to get going. The best shooting in this field is going to be right at first light. And we won't get two chances."

He was still in his shorts, had all the lanterns on in camp – it looked like a new car dealership opening up – and was madly boiling two pots of water.

"What in the hell are you doing?" I fumed. "We gotta haul ass."

Then the big mirror came out. I couldn't believe it. It's time for the shoot and he's cleaning up. This guy hadn't spent a whole lot of time in Baja before, that was for sure.

"I'm putting in my contacts."

"Oh, for Christ's sake."

"You go on. I'll be right down."

I didn't need that invitation twice. I hoofed it back down the field and just at first light, grabbed my gun, two ammo belts, and slogged out into the mud. No two ways about it. This was going to be messy *and* cold. When I got out about a hundred yards from the now completely flooded dirt road, I picked a likely row and eased down into the mud and water, being sure to keep my gun and ammo clean and dry. No sooner was I set than bingo, in they came. Hundreds of teal were looking over the few dekes I had thrown out around me. But they *knew* there was seed in this field. That's why the Mexicans irrigated it. They piled in, pairs and triplets, larger flights, and occasionally, truly huge, hundred bird flights. I looked down the road and still no Herb. I couldn't wait any longer. *"Bam, bam, bablam, bam, bam."* Two folded, a teal and something else, but it was too dark to tell; Sprig, I think. The birds feeding didn't even bother to get up. I didn't spook 'em at all. Oh boy, oh boy, oh boy! This was going to be a lulu. *"Blam, Bam. Splash.."* Then farther away, there was another *"splash.."* Another pair. Wow! This was hot. A flight of widgeon whistling *"whe-whew, whe-whew, whe-whew,"* came in for a look, and I stayed down while they deked in. That's when I noticed. My gun was full of mud. The pump ejection mechanism had mud everywhere; my shell belt was completely mudded up. Hell, I couldn't put those shells through the barrel. It'd blow up. I needed a new approach, besides which my legs and chest were wet and frozen. In the distance I spotted Herb. This place was now getting unhuntable. I couldn't lie in the mud and conceal myself without fouling all my ammo and gun.

Herb came up to the roadside bush where I had left his gun and ammo, and two sacks of dekes.

"I'm gonna pull these dekes, and we'll have to see how much cover that *chamiso* gives us," I shouted.

He nodded his approval, and went about shoring up the *chamiso* so that we could use it for cover. I threw out the few dekes I had brought in from the field, and emptied another sack besides.

"Get down," he said. "Incoming."

I finished putting out the dekes, then staggered back in through the slop. Two gadwall wanted in and I was still standing in the open. *"Boom, boom."*

"Nice double," I yelled.

Herb beamed. "C'mon, get out of the field."

After that it was continuous action until dark. We never had more than fifteen minutes between flights of ducks, all wanting to get into our flooded field. Not all of them came in, but my sprig whistle sure turned a bunch of 'em. About mid-day Herb had eaten all the Baby Ruths, Butterfingers, and Three Musketeers. Also three cokes. During several breaks in the action, I got out and photographed Herb in the *chamiso* bush. I swear the blind was so good I couldn't really see him; just maybe a glint off his gun barrel gave him away. For Herb, it was a time-of-your-life duck shoot. The limits in the U.S. had been lowered long ago, and it was a special occasion to be in on a duck shoot like this.

One other thing I noticed. When I shot, the birds didn't fall; when Herb shot, they did. That happens sometimes. Your shooting eye just deserts you. You never know when its gonna happen and *bang*, there it is. For my part, just seeing the ducks decoy in, hearing the guns go off, being in the great outdoors – in a wilderness, no less – those were the things I loved; that and the campfire-cooked food, Tecate quart beers – that's what this was all about.

"*Baboom, boom!* There's fifty. That's the limit, twenty-five each." Herb was excited. Really excited.

We had thrown all the ducks in a pile, but Herb had counted. "Thirty-six," he said proudly. That meant I had fourteen, not bad by American standards; but Herb had outshot me three to one. Who would have 'thunk' it? We loaded up the ducks on duck straps, shouldered the decoy bags, and headed back to camp. It was just dusk, so we put the ducks in the Blazer, along with the beans and rice, and headed over to Lupe's.

"*Buenas noches. Buen tiro?*" asked Don Emilio.

They could hear the shooting all day, so they knew we'd had one helluva hunt. I unloaded the ducks on the table, and Don Emilio gave us a big smile. "*Pueden a limpiarlos?*" I asked him.

"*Sí, como no.*" he answered. With that the ducks were taken away. The whole family would be gutting and feathering ducks tonight. And did they ever do a good job.

"*Mamacita, tenemos unas cosas para ustedes. Viene.*"

She went with us to the Blazer and when she saw the 100 pound rice and bean bags, a wonderful smile lit up her face.

"*Gracias*, Larri."

Then Herb brought out the coffee, and I thought he might get his first Mexican kiss. Mamacita was very gracious, accepted the coffee, and then offered us some *tortillas* and *frijoles*.

Herb declined, but after my third helping, he said, "Well, maybe just a little bit."

Five helpings and several quarts of Tecate later, Herb asked me to tell mamacita that it was really good.

"Better than Taco Bell?" I asked. He had to think about that one.

I introduced Herb around, and after a while he asked, "Where do all these people live?"

"In the house."

"All of 'em?"

"Yep. Lupe, Yolanda, el Señor, Don Emilio, Mamacita, Roberto, and two or three grandkids. They all live here."

"Boy, they must all know one another pretty well then." There was a lot of truth to that.

"Is this the kitchen?" he asked, pointing to where the beans and tortillas kept appearing from.

"Yeah. You want to go in and get warm?"

Herb was bug-eyed. A little dried mud brick oven and steel sheet made up the stove. "Where's the ice box?"

"There is none. No electricity." The *electrificada rural* still hadn't made it to Lupe's.

"How can you live without an ice box out here?"

"Lots of trips to town and no perishables."

Herb was impressed. "Now you see part of the reason they exist on tortillas and beans; that and the fact that they love 'em."

Herb had seen lots of things while in the Highway Patrol; but nothing had prepared him for this. I could see he was mentally counting his blessings. A little reality testing was good for us all, now and again. A bit later we called it a night. Tomorrow I had planned to meet up with Barr, an old hunting buddy from internship days. He was coming down to Baja in his big brand new Ford F250 pick-up, and was dying to show it off. If all went as I planned tomorrow, he'd get plenty of opportunity. Actually I had expected him last night. He would have gotten a real kick in the pants from our field shoot. Before leaving, I told Don Emilio that if Barr got here after we left, to send him over towards the lagoons out behind Luis B. Encinas.

"*Bueno,* Larri; *Buenas noches, y gracias.*"

I was so stuffed from Mamacita's *tortillas* and beans that I didn't need any dinner; same for Herb. So we called it a night, loaded the boat on the Blazer, put dekes, ammo and cleaned guns inside, then sacked out. I hoped Barr would join us tonight, but if not, he'd know the general area where we'd be deked out.

Luis B. Encinas was a ways, probably 30 to 45 minutes if no roads were flooded and I didn't get lost. Getting Herb going was a snap this time; he'd really had his appetite whetted in that field shoot. He asked no less than ten thousand questions before we got there, not the least of which was, "Why didn't we go back and hunt the field again?"

"Because if you return the following day, nothing will be there. It takes at least four days before ducks will return to where they've been shot at; and in this case, the field will be dry by then, so we got the one and only field shoot that place will give up this year."

We got lost twice en route to Luis B. Encinas. I was used to getting there in the daylight, but with flooded fields, you sometimes have to make your own roads, just as the Mexicans do. We found the landmark Luis B. Encinas water tower right at dawn. That was the good news. The rest of the news was that to get to the ponds south of town, we were going to have to walk, as the dirt road was completely under water. It was only a couple of miles, but that meant no boat. Rather than hike out there with full gear, we decided to go reconnoiter first, and then decide what to do. About half way out, a '58 Chevy running four slicks came slipping and sliding down the road and in the field – all the way out to the fish camp on the ponds. We turned around, sprinted back to the Blazer, put her in four-wheel-drive, and were off. Having watched the locals do this for years, I knew the trick was to go real slow, let the tires spin until they got down to hard, dry dirt below, and off you go. We did exactly that and covered the two miles in just under thirty minutes. Our tire tracks, however, made it look like someone had driven a tractor – a very large tractor – through the roads, and completely chewed them up. It had to be our huge oversized Armstrong mud tires. They got us there, but every bit of mud they threw up ended up somewhere in, on, or beneath the Blazer. When we stopped, vehicle color, make, even size and shape were obscured. It looked like a big, brown, square, mud glob with two shiny eyes where the windshield wipers and sprayers had kept the windshield un-mudded. I was disappointed in Barr not being here; he would have loved this. Just not in his brand new truck. I left word at the adobe hut nearest the road, to tell Barr we were out at the ponds. But that was superfluous – if he saw those big tire tracks going through the submerged road, he'd know who it was.

In the meantime, Herb and I checked out the tules and ponds, and although we didn't see much, it was obvious there were some ducks out there. We launched the boat, loaded her up and set out, heading southwest, towards some bigger water. We found a relatively good flyway, deked it, and two hours later, had limited out. I brought my shooting eye today, and managed to give old Herb a few lessons.

As we chugged back in, we could see a moving mud storm coming down the road. Barr! And he was motoring. Mud flying everywhere. We could see it even a half mile off – fishtailing, motor racing, tires spinning, 180°'s, 360°'s, the whole shot. It was amazing to watch. He had told me his new beauty was green, so to look for it. But half way there, he was completely mudded over, except for the two clear glass eyeballs in the windshield. We got to the bank just a hair before Barr, and watched in amazement as he traversed the last couple hundred yards.

"Geez, we musta' looked just like that," exclaimed Herb.

"Yeah."

Barr arrived, draped his hands over the steering wheel, put his head on his hands, and looked like he was wiped out. Jesus! Huh? Do you believe this? Nobody can come through mud like that, nobody! When I saw those tracks, though, I knew it was you, Stanton. You've got to be crazy!"

Then he got out, looked at the Blazer, and just laughed and laughed. "God, look at this thing. Solid mud everywhere. You're nuts." Then it hit him. He turned and looked at the new F250. "Oh my God, oh my God. It's ruined, it's ruined, my new 250 is ruined. Stanton, you crazy bastard. You've made me ruin my new truck." He was visibly anguished.

"Hey, Ron, good to see you," and I went over and gave him a big hug.

He looked at the two trucks for another few moments, then exclaimed, "Well, I guess you ruined yours too."

"What do you mean? That's not *my* truck. That's the ex-wife's. She let me borrow it. I wouldn't bring my own truck in here. Have to be crazy to do that."

We all got a laugh out of that, and then after introductions, we brought out some Tecate quarts. In short order, Barr had inspected the duck stringers in the boat, and was ready to go. We convinced him otherwise, because we had already pretty well shot out the area. He was crestfallen. When we told him about the field shoot the day before, he felt worse, but was anxious to go there and see if any ducks had come back in. We loaded up, then headed back to Luis B. Encinas. This time we drove through flooded open fields, fishtailing, spinning, but always slowly moving onward. Barr was behind us, and said later that night that it just didn't seem possible to get through muddy fields like that. We got back to camp, unloaded, and took Mamacita our second haul of ducks. Barr went and checked out the field, and saw enough to make him want to try it in the morning. In the meantime, I suggested we go try and scare up some quail. There was no wind, it was just the perfect time in the afternoon, and it was only the second day of the season.

We scared up several coveys and got a nice bunch of birds for dinner. I would flour these babies up with rosemary and thyme, then add a pinch of garlic salt, quick fry in oil and *voilá*, a meal for the gods. Herb brought out the bottle of tequila, Sauza Commemorativo, my favorite, and we celebrated. Couple swigs each, then a Tecate, couple more swigs, and a few short minutes later I was swacked. We were on the schoolhouse road, so we were only 15 minutes from camp. I took the Blazer over the first dike – too fast – and we bounced down on the other side, then did a 360° and followed that up by sliding backwards, 30 yards down the muddy road. All of a sudden a *"Whirrrrr, clank, bang, whirr,"* and smoke started coming out from under the hood. I got out, took two steps, and threw up. Barr pulled up behind us, just as Herb had managed to get the hood open. With the engine off, the whirring continued. Herb somehow figured that the electric winch had shorted out and was in the process of burning up the winch motor. It was also in the process of bending the front grill to pieces. He disconnected the battery cables and it stopped. Barr came over, looked at the mud covering the engine, winch, carburetor, radiator, and exclaimed, "Hey, that's great. As long as you don't reconnect your battery, you're fine."

I laid on my stomach in the mud and tried not to move. Barr came over. "How 'bout some more tequila? Stanton you are green. Your whole face is green. You look like hell."

"Barf. Baarrff." My only two responses.

They worked on the winch a while and finally Herb figured it out. Further examination revealed that the winch motor had been shorted out by the solid mud encasing it. "Stanton, the only thing you're gonna be able to do with this rig is torch it and hope the insurance covers it. It is destroyed."

"Barf. Barf."

They loaded me up, and we headed back to camp. Following my recipe instructions, the boys fixed up a nice bunch of quail. I tried to eat some to soak up that damn tequila, but they just came back up. "Good job, Stanton," was all Barr could say, laughing at me heaving into the garbage pile.

Later that night the dizziness stopped and there was that brief moment when I thought I might still want to live after all. Then it came back again, just as I deserved. That was the last drunk I allowed myself. Ever! Nothing could be worth this. It was funny; in the old days a bottle of tequila and a quart of Tecate wouldn't have touched me. But it did now. Wow, did it ever!

Next morning I didn't take the wake-up call, but heard the boys shooting occasionally over in the flooded field. Before leaving, Barr tried the strongarm tactics to get me out of the sack, but I told him I had the feeling camp was the place to be. I joked that if he heard a lot of shooting near camp, to come on back. "Very funny," was the reply.

After they were gone, I got up and made coffee, and watched as rain clouds gathered overhead. In Baja, rain is a very unusual occurrence. During the 300 or more trips I have made to Baja, it has rained exactly twice. But thunderheads formed rapidly as I watched, and soon it started to rain; exactly at that moment the dove flight started over the tent. It was a joke. Birds by the hundreds, all flying right over the tamarack; there were hundreds of thousands of square miles over which they could pass, but they chose our campsite. Not disappointed, I put on a pair of underwear, brought out a campstool, sat down and loaded up. Then that magical sound – *"boom, boom, ba-boom, boom, boom."* In ten minutes I shot a box of shells, reloaded and promptly went through another. The shooting was hot and continuous. The rain was falling pretty steadily by then, so every time I went to retrieve a dove, adobe mud caked up on the bottom of my bare feet.

Soon Herb and Barr returned to find out what all the

shooting was about. Over the next hour we shot a case of shells between the three of us, and had a pile of birds for ourselves, plus a good-sized contribution towards chili colorado. During the shooting, we didn't talk much, but there were lots of expletives, squeals, laughter, and "*Behind you, over,* and *high rights.*" Barr didn't get his duck shoot but he sure got his fill of doves.

Afterwards, Barr began telling stories which we all enjoyed. Most of 'em I'd heard before, but with each retelling, they came out better. His eyes kept glancing back at the F250, however, and it was plain that he wondered how he could possibly get his new truck clean. I told him about the car wash in Estacion Coahuila, manual of course, and suggested that after breaking camp, we both go by there. Barr looked skeptical. "Why would there be a car wash in a town that had no paved roads?" he wondered aloud.

That was a reasonable question, but I just repeated that I had seen a car wash just past Coahuila near Riito. By noon we had had our chili colorado doves, and had said our goodbyes at Lupe's. As usual, they wanted to know when we'd be back; I was uncertain, but probably in late January, I guessed. We followed the back roads into Coahuila, found the car wash, complete with nine little boys with buckets and soapy water. I conferred with them and we established a price, two dollars as I recall, and away they went. Barr was kind of non-plussed, but decided to leave his truck anyway. To kill time we walked around Coahuila. Herb had never seen anything like it. Anything you wanted, you could buy here. It was just that nothing was new, and one size fit all – and if not, it was rapidly converted to fit by deft Mexican craftsmen.

A quick stop at the Tecate parlor, and we headed back to the car "wash." When we returned, both trucks were mud free, spit polish clean. Barr went over to inspect his truck and seeing no water spilled on the ground, inquired how they got it so clean.'

"*Con estos,*" they replied, lifting up their cleaning sticks.

A nude Curran chows down after an unbelievable morning hunt in the swamp. Back then the limit was 50 birds per day and we had set up right in their flight path.

My good friend Palmer three days out of submarine school and just back from the morning's duck hunt. He was supposed to be helping me clean ducks, but couldn't resist these two beauties right next to camp.

This is Don Emilio and his family, Roberto, Mamacita, Lupe and the girls, Ynez, Hilda and Rita. These folks became good friends and helped us out of many a jam. We reciprocated by bringing down clothing, food and sometimes providing medical care. We also put on Lupe's wedding.

Lupe's grandfather, El Señor, and one of his many grand-daughters, Ynez. He was 118 years old here and had fascinating tales to tell about Pancho Villa and other legendary banditos. He ate tortillas and beans every meal and lived to age 125. I have since added lots of beans and tortillas to my diet!

The helicopter was the only way into this canyon and the trout fishing was as spectacular as the scenery. We had to make three trips to get the gear, etc. in there. Thank God I only had to go once!

Desert quail are a kick in the pants! I know I shouldn't be shooting quail with a 12-gauge automatic, but the authorities only allowed one gun per season per hunter back then, so one must make do. Besides, I grew up in Texas and Texans will shoot 'em with anything!

Curran already had the grease hot when this picture was made and since he was the cook, guess who had to clean the quail! The action that day was like a dream, short brush, birds held well and they flushed in only pairs and trips.

Below: This little channel extended right out into the desert from the Rio Colorado. Cindy looks a little worried here, as if she might have to pull the boat out to Duarte pond and back. She was right!

Curran and our artistic rendition of a dead duck photo. This mixed bag included redheads, sprig, gadwall and teal. The two I shot are in the far right front. When you were shooting with Mike you not only had to shoot straight, you had to shoot fast!

Ron was apoplectic.

"You cleaned the mud off my truck with wooden sticks? This is a brand new truck, new paint job, and you scraped the mud off with sticks?"

But when you looked at it, they had done a magnificent job.

Both vehicles shone in the noonday sun, and try as he might, Barr could find no stick scratches on his truck. We said our goodbyes, loaded up, and just before heading out, Ron stuck his head out the window and said, "Stanton, I dunno. I think I'm just getting too old for this stuff."

He'd be back – but I doubted he'd bring his beloved F250, though.

Clay

'mon, Stanton! Tell the story about the west Texas
hunt. C'mon."

"Barr, you've heard that damn story half a dozen
times, it hasn't changed any, and what's more, you
tell it better than I do."

"Hey, it gets better every time. I just love hearing that
story."

"Anybody want more pheasant?" I asked, passing
around the platter.

"No, but I'll take another Tecate," added Braith.

"Tecate all around then," and Barr, Nold, Curran and I
all helped ourselves to icy cold quarts. There is *nothing*
better than rosemary and thyme fried pheasant with a
quart bottle of Tecate. Nothing.

"Stanton, I'll do dishes if you'll tell it. I wouldn't mind
hearing it again either," offered Braith.

"Okay you guys, but remember you asked me." I had
told this story a number of times before, but Barr always
got me going again.

"Well, during spring break of sophomore year at *The
University* – that's the University of Texas at Austin, for
those of you who might not have recognized *The
University* – a guy who lived down the hall invited my
roommate and me down to his dad's ranch in Laredo
County in southwest Texas. Fred, my roommate, begged

off, as he was once again in love. For young Fred it didn't take much, as he fell in love with any woman who smiled at him. "No, I'll pass, Yank," he told me. "Got this sweet young thing and I think I'm in love."

"Again, Y.F.?"

"Hey, she looked at me, okay? If she's not interested, she wouldn't be looking at me, right?"

"Fred, didn't you just meet her this morning?"

"Yeah, in Econ 101 class."

"But don't you think it's just a bit much to take her for a spring break skiing trip to Vail, for a week, when you just met her this morning?"

"Did you ask her yet, Fred?" chimed in Johnny Bob.

"No, but I know she'll go."

"How do you know that?"

"Look, I just have a feeling, all right? She looked at me, she'll go."

That was the conversation I remembered as we were cruising southwest, with the top down and cowboy tunes blaring from the car radio. I looked over at Clay once again, and wondered how I had gotten myself into this. Clay was Fred's friend, not mine; heck, I hardly knew him. Seen him around the dorm a few times, but he seemed kinda quiet, and kept to himself. What he was doing living in the athletic dorm was a real mystery. I mean, he had coke bottle glasses, pimples all over his face, he was short and skinny with a sunken-in chest and . . . he had a *car*, not to mention his father's ranch. No, Clay was not your typical suave, debonair Texan. He was more like . . . well, he was more like a . . . *geek*. He was nice enough, but seemed kind of immature for a second year college student.

We had the convertible top down the whole way, so there was not much conversation. If you've ever driven this area, you know there are miles and miles of miles and miles. The farther south we went, the more desolate and desert-like the countryside became. At dark, we were still headed south, and I figured we must be close, as signs pointing towards Laredo read, "Laredo 30 miles." I was mildly surprised when we got to the border and ended up crossing.

"You didn't say your dad's ranch was on the Mexican side."

"It's not."

"What're we doing down here, then?"

"*Poontang*, man. Some of the best hot stuff you'll ever lay eyes on. And they just love us *gringos*."

Ah ha. The reason for my invitation to Clay's ranch was becoming clearer; Clay didn't want to go to the whorehouse alone.

"Been down here quite a few times have you?"

"Oh yeah," he said, but I doubted it. "I come here all the time. Everybody knows *Papagallos*."

He was right about that. There were some great stories from *Papagallos*, where many a young boy entered, then later left, thinking he was a man. Everything was done in blue – the bar, the curtains, the individual one room "*casitas*"out back for the ladies. The "little houses" were arranged in a semicircular fashion, with a central grassy area, complete with hose bibb and hose, so the girls could douche after each customer. Clay couldn't decide which of the girls that came to the table he wanted, so he took all three. That came to a total of fifteen bucks — twenty if you included his one five dollar Cuba Libre. I told the ladies at my table, "*Gracias, no*, I was just waiting for my friend."

Half an hour later, this buxom dark-eyed honey came back and said, "*Señor*, you've had fifteen dollars worth of drinks. Are you sure you wouldn't like five dollars worth of pleasure?"

Still no Clay, so what the heck. "Why not? You bet," I said, as we went in back to her *casita*. First thing she did was go over to the hose, bent over, and douched. Clay's idea of romance didn't quite seem on the same track as mine. She came back to the *casita*, undressed me and I succumbed to power failure. Since I had already paid my five dollars, she was going to see to it that I got my money's worth. Besides, as she put it, I was cute and she thought she might be in love. All I can remember is thinking "This is like trying to nail two boards together with a piece of spaghetti."

Ultimately, she gave up, or more likely my time ran out. Clay was back in the bar, with a big grin on his face, and an empty bottle of Old Crow on the table. If *three sheets to the wind* constitutes a drunk, Clay was two-thirds of the way there. "C'mon *amigo*," I said, helping him out of his chair.

Papagallos had guarded our car while we were inside. Locals didn't mess with customer's cars there; it was bad for business. We got in, uneventfully drove back through town, crossed the border checkpoint, and drove off into the South Texas night. A mile out of town, Clay reached under the seat and produced an unopened bottle of Old Crow.

"Where'd you get that?"

"Back at Papagallos," he answered.

"You idiot. You realize what those *gringo* border guards do if you sneak hard liquor back across the border? Hell, they impound your car, put you in jail and throw away the key. They don't screw around with liquor laws in Texas. They've got one heck of a liquor lobby here."

"Yeah, but they *didn't* catch us, and we're headed home. Have a drink."

We drove perhaps another hour or so, and saw so many stars it just hurt our eyes. There were no lights, no buildings, no civilization; here there was only beauty and serenity. At some point we turned off the highway and entered the ranch. The gravel crunched on the road which dipped and dove through the various washes and *arroyos*. As we rounded one corner, there were a dozen deer, frozen in the headlights. They let us drive right up to them, then startled, bounded away. Another forty five minutes and we were there.

Clay was barely able to stagger in, so I helped him into

the ranch house. It was small and compact, with a shiny tin roof, a small but adequate kitchen, a bedroom set immediately behind, and, of course, the trademark west Texas front porch, complete with rocking chairs. All in all a neat little setup; low budget, but efficient. This served as a bunk house when Clay's dad came down to hunt deer or to check on his prize cattle herd. Of the two beds, Clay chose the one closest to the window; he took out my shotgun, loaded up, and laid it down beside him. He muttered something about *bandidos*, but I didn't catch it all. Then before going to sleep he said something about the outhouse out back, and "take the pistol with you," motioning to a holstered revolver up on the wall. With that, he was out, and I didn't hear from him again that night. I remember looking out the window a while, then I dozed off also.

Several hours later some stomach pangs awoke me. Musta' been that salsa they served with those chips back at Papagallos. I found the flashlight, strapped on the pearl-handled Colt 45, then headed off to the crapper. Halfway there, I spotted them, dozens of pairs of orange eyes reflected in the flashlight. There must have been a hundred coyotes out there and it looked like they were coming after me. I drew the pistol and put six quick shots in the general direction of the eyes. I heard some thuds and some coyote howls, but bare-assed naked with a pair of boots and a gunbelt on, I had suddenly lost the urge to use the outhouse. Slowly, I walked back towards the ranch house, checking in back every so many steps, to make sure the coyotes didn't attack me from behind. I remembered hearing some shots find their mark with a thud, so I felt a little safer on the way back in. The outhouse was beginning to look like a daylight trip.

Back in the bunkhouse I managed to get back to bed without waking Clay, though it was hard to believe he hadn't heard my shots. No sound came from his bed. Sometime later when my heart rate came back down, I dropped back off to sleep. I was awakened sometime after dawn by a *"tat-tat-tat-tat; tat-tat-tat-tat."* Then silence, then again, *"tat-tat-tat. Tat . . . tat-tat-tat"*. Opening one eye, I could see a woodpecker cracking nuts on the roof above for all he was worth. I drifted in and out of sleep several times, when it began again. *"Tat-tat. Tat-BOOM."* A gun shot went off right next to my ear; that shot me straight up in bed. God, that was close. Shattered glass was all over the room, the window was blown out, and the roof edge had a big chunk missing. No more woodpecker, either. Clay had set my smoking shotgun down next to his bed after shooting out the window and was already back asleep. Once again, the outhouse idea was starting to sound good.

After putting on boots, I went back outside, sans pistol this time. The outhouse was a standard one-holer – I've always wondered what kind of people sat on two-holers. Opening the door, my heart sank. I saw what the thuds were from last night. Four shots had struck home – two right through the door, one through the lateral door frame, cutting the 2"x4" neatly in half, and the fourth through the upper door frame. It was an old outhouse made of barn-wood, and was extremely fragile looking. The two frame shots made it cant slightly to the left, forcing the door open. The door holes had converted this into an open air crapper, as the .45 caliber hollowpoint bullets had blown apart upon hitting the wood, leaving little, indeed, of the front door. Those same two bullets had hit the seat board and all around the hole were chewed up splinters of wood. It appeared that if you sat on it, you would almost certainly fall through. The bullets had fragmented so badly by the time they reached the back of the outhouse that there was no back. You could see for miles through the back. Cautiously, I closed the door, walked behind the ruined structure, squatted down, and got rid of that salsa – near the outhouse, just not quite in it. I kicked dirt over the leavings, then headed back. No point in waking Clay; he'd certainly see it when he got up.

I fixed some breakfast, canned beans and tamales, then

went back to get Clay up, but he was unarousable. I picked up the .270, put it in the jeep, and headed out. In the daylight, you could see the thought that had gone into the choice of the ranch house site. You actually had to drive down into an arroyo, then up the other side to get to the house. It was on a hillock, surrounded by an arroyo. It would always be above water, even during a flash flood. There was a jeep at the ranch house, covered with a tarp, which upon inspection, looked to be in good working order. Clay had mentioned last evening that there was a Mexican foreman who watched the cattle and ranch house and kept the jeep battery charged. Sure enough, she fired right up, and I was gone. It took a few minutes to figure out the four wheel drive business, but minutes later I was four-wheeling all over that ranch, blazing new pathways as I went.

The vegetation was west Texas scrub, or *chamiso*, with no trees. There was enough for the cattle to eat, but it was certain they had to work for it. I came across huge vultures, rabbits, several coyotes at a great distance, some cow pies, but no cattle. Clay had said this was his dad's *big* ranch. There were two others, but they were nowhere near the size of this one. He thought this ranch was something like thirty five miles long, and almost twenty in width. Seven hundred square miles is a big ranch, even in Texas.

There were some quail, but I only saw a few birds once, not thereafter. I stopped near a cactus and test fired the .270, to get a better idea of how far it dropped over a hundred yards. It seemed pretty flat shooting, so the bullets must have been at least 180 grain. After the two test fires, however, the bunnies had me figured out, and associated the jeep with the hunter; they disappeared also. Just four-wheeling around the ranch, however, proved to be terrific fun. I'd go down an arroyo and up the other side, all four tires off the ground, and *crash*, touch down and be off again. After three hours of this, I was ready to head back. I did some donuts, and noticed there was a small leak trailing the jeep. Didn't seem to be bad, so I ignored it and headed in.

I was probably ten miles from the house, and made the trip back in record time, four-wheeling over anything and everything that got in my way. When I came to the arroyo surrounding the cabin, I accelerated down in and came flying up the other side. As I hit the brakes my foot went straight to the floorboard. The thought of the leaking fluid flashed through my mind just as I crashed into the porch, chugged through the front door, into the kitchen, and kept chugging, pushing the ice box into the bedroom. Finally, the collapsed cabinets, ice box, kitchen table, chairs, and the bedroom doorjam stopped the jeep. It happened so fast that I hadn't had the presence of mind to turn off the ignition. The porch roof had fallen down behind me, the kitchen roof had fallen down on me, the table was in pieces under the front wheels, the fallen canned goods had broken the windshield, and the dented-in ice box was bashed open, now in the bedroom next to Clay's bed. He had gotten up, but was so hung over, he couldn't grasp the situation. Several minutes later, however, he did, and he started to howl like a wounded bear.

"Oh jeez, oh God, oh jeez, oh man, oh my gosh! Oh I don't believe it. Oh no, oh no. What happened? Oh gosh, I can't believe it! What a mess. What happened? Larry, what happened?"

I just kinda shrugged and said, "The jeep."

You didn't have to be a rocket scientist to figure out the rest: porch gone, kitchen gone, roof gone, table gone, ice box gone. And Clay had shot out the bedroom window. The ranch house reminded me vaguely of a piece of swiss cheese that had just been stepped on by a horse.

"Oh man. Well, what're we going to do? Get the jeep out, I guess, if we want to go hunting. I think I'm going to eat first, though." And with that Clay sat down on his bunk and opened the ice box door, now conveniently located next to his bed. Breakfast for him consisted of two beers sandwiched around some cold V-8. He tore down that part of the kitchen wall that wasn't already in the bed-room, found a can of peas that was on the floor, and ate that. Under the jeep was a can of rhubarb, and that was next. Then he found a jar of Vienna sausages and ate that. Whew! This guy knew how to eat. Like he said, "It was a balanced meal with a selection from each of the three food groups – beer, cans, and bottles."

Cleaning up after breakfast seemed superfluous. You know, what's a couple of empty cans and bottles thrown on the floor going to hurt when you've caved in half the house, right? And besides, Clay assured me, Jose, the Mexican foreman, was real handy and he'd be able to fix everything.

"Right," I thought. "All he needs is fifteen thousand dollars and about four months." But I kept those thoughts to myself. Clay was already making plans for another whorehouse raid tonight, and at the thought of it, his spirits brightened markedly.

We put a rope on the jeep's trailer hitch and pulled it out with the convertible. Aside from the broken windshield, there were no other problems . . . unless you include the no brakes business. Clay had a battle plan for the day that culminated in hunting one of those monster-sized vultures. First, however, we needed something dead for bait; that's where the bunnies came in. So off we went with a .22 and 12 gauge in search of the elusive wild Texas jacks. Clay knew where there was a passel of them about an hour and a half away. Lord, were there ever – bunnies everywhere. I picked up the Beretta, jacked five shells in and let fly. Incredibly, I missed everything. I had thought these guys were easy to hit. Four shells later, nothing; another three shots and the same. Frustrated and impatient, Clay grabbed my gun. "Here, give me that damn thing," and on his first shot, three unfortunates somehow managed to line themselves up and he dropped all three with one shell. I know full well he couldn't do that again in *six* lifetimes; but it was impressive nonetheless.

We shot several more, then took them to the highest mound we could find, laid them in a pile, and drove off about a mile. Clay said we'd not need field glasses because we'd be able to tell when the vultures landed. Half an hour later, they had spotted the bait and were circling in earnest. We sucked down a couple of beers, and Clay recounted the previous night's happenings, but mainly, we just waited. It wasn't long, for no sooner had the buzzards begun to circle, than they rapidly descended and got down to the serious business of eating dead bunnies.

We watched as two dozen lit, then waited awhile for them to really get the blood taste in their mouths. An hour later, Clay revved up the jeep and off we went. I was *riding shotgun* – holding the Beretta with five shells in the magazine and chamber, in my hand; for the first time I understood where that term had come from. Our plan was to drive straight at them, and last bird up, concentrate on him. As we neared the dead rabbits, the buzzards took off, several staying a bit longer than others. Finally, the last bird jumped up and the chase was on. At sixty yards I pumped some high base 6's in him; at forty, two more direct hits. But these birds are mean and tough, and this fellow kept going. At twenty yards, I put it right on his head, a direct hit, but on he went. At ten, another head shot, but he still flew, although now, much lower. The jeep was bouncing around so badly I hadn't been able to reload. Clay stayed on him, and as we came up alongside, I whacked him with the gun barrel. Another swing connected and down he went, dead as a stone. By rights, he should have been dead half a mile back. We pulled the jeep up along side him, and got out for the victory pictures. Clay held the buzzard up first. The wing span looked to be at least seven feet. He stretched the wings out and held him like that awhile, as I photographed it. Then we traded places. Clay had the camera and I held the buzzard up, showing off the remarkable wing span. Just as Clay snapped the picture, the buzzard raised his head up and vomited on me in one last defiant gesture. Oh was that foul! Decaying meat from the last two or three days, in various stages of decomposition, was all over my shoes, pants, shirt and arms. What a stink! I took off the clothes and left them, but the stench would not come off the arms. As bad as I smelled, I prevailed upon Clay to return to the ranch house and let me clean up, and also get some clothes.

Well, I cleaned up, but the buzzard had the last laugh. That smell did not come out. It was grim. It was the only thing I could think about because of the overpowering odor. Nothing worked, so finally Clay said to forget it and we'd go back out hunting – for deer, he grinned.

"But it isn't season and you don't have a license," I pointed out.

"On your own ranch, you can do whatever you want," he replied.

Well, I wasn't about to argue the fish and game laws with him, but I knew for certain he was wrong. "You're the hunter, boss," I said, as I fervently hoped they wouldn't put me in jail with him when they caught us; but I knew differently.

We bounced along over ridges, arroyos, into thick cover and out again. At this time of day there wasn't that much game to see. I mentioned to Clay that until closer towards evening, there really wouldn't be much deer sighting. He jumped on the brakes, pointed along the western horizon, and said, "Oh no?"

I could barely see it, but there was, in fact, a silhouette in that direction; I just couldn't make it out. "It's a buck," exclaimed Clay joyously.

"Wanna stalk it?"

"Heck no. I can drop that beauty from here."

He had been lucky once today with the shotgun. It wouldn't happen twice. "*Ba-boom*," shattered the desert stillness.

"Got him," exulted Clay.

"No way."

"You see a silhouette on that horizon?" he shouted.

Well I looked, but it was so far, I just couldn't tell. "I dunno," was all I could manage.

"I got him, I know I got him."

And off we went, bumping over the desert and *chamiso* unhealthily fast. We came to an arroyo, descended into it, then came up the other side, just about where that buck should have been. As we crowned, Clay's eyes got big as saucers and he said, "Oh, my God. I shot Jack." And there before us, exhaling his last breath, lay Big Jack, the prize bull of his dad's herd.

"Oh no. Oh no, oh no, no, no. We couldn't have killed Jack. Oh nooooo."

"We?"

"Well, you know, we are kinda together in this."

"Right, Clay."

"Oh what are we going to do?"

"Just looking at him, I'd say he'd make some mighty fine steaks. And I've got my butchering knife on me."

"Oh no, we can't do that. We've got to hide him, leave no traces."

"Hide him?"

"Yeah, you know, hide him."

With that, Clay was rummaging through the jeep tool kit and came up with a folding foxhole spade, pulled her out, and began digging the largest manually dug hole I had ever seen. He worked feverishly, glancing furtively behind him every few minutes, hoping against hope that the Mexican foreman would not happen upon us. In thirty minutes he had dug a hole as big as a grave. An hour later, and he had one big enough for Jack. Rolling him in turned out to be a challenge, so Clay hooked him up to the jeep rope and pulled Big Jack in.

"Clay, are you sure I can't take just a few steaks? I mean, what a waste just to bury him."

"No, dammit, now don't ask again."

With that he grabbed the shovel and had Big Jack

buried forty-five minutes later. As long as I live I will never forget that sight – this skinny kid digging a hole for this huge twelve hundred pound bull, then burying him in it. When he finished, it was just dark, and I was ready to go back to the ranch house and hit the sack.

When I suggested it to Clay, he looked indignant, then said we were outta here. And he meant west Texas. We drove back to the house, changed cars, got in the convertible and we were history. No stopping at the whorehouse, no dinner, no *nada*. We just high-tailed it for home.

When we got back to Austin, we bagged it and slept most of the next day. I didn't see Clay much after that until about a week later. His door was open and he was on the phone, gesticulating with his hands. I went in to say hello, but he didn't notice me. He was obviously listening to a long tirade from the other end, and looked plenty upset about it. I waited a minute, then sensing I was intruding, got up to leave. The very last thing I heard was "Oh, no sir. We may have caused a little damage to the cabin, but no sir, we don't know anything about Big Jack. You have my word on that, sir."

"Well, boys, that about does it for me. Need to be up at three-thirty if we're gonna make it to the south end of the big pond by first light. I'm turnin' in. Thanks for doin' the dishes. Don't mind cooking the pheasant, but sure a pain to clean up after."

But the words fell on deaf ears. Braith and Barr were fast asleep, fully clothed, ready for the morning hunt. Barr had curled up by the fire and Braith had just leaned back against the old adobe wall and passed out. The Tecate was long gone, the west Texas story was told, but the dishes... well, two out of three wasn't so bad.

Jacke

I rolled into Sombrerete at dusk, just a little over five hours after leaving Huntington Beach. This was a near record, as usually we pulled into the hunting areas closer to dawn. Turning down schoolhouse road there were the usual little kids playing in the mud, having stick fights, tending goats, or just hanging out. Once past the few adobe homes congregated at the corner, the number of dwellings along the road thinned out; schoolhouse road was a straight fifteen mile shot to Duarte pond, and there were only two houses along the way. It was cold already, typical for late December, and I hadn't been down since the last fiasco. The wife and I had been down then. We had left the kids at home with Brenda, the babysitter, and had taken off for three days of camping and hunting. The only dicey part was that I was recovering from reconstructive knee surgery, and had been away from my dermatology residency for six weeks already. I planned to return after our three day Baja trip. Unfortunately, when we got back, Brenda informed me that my chief, Dr. Wilson, had called to check on my progress. During the course of the conversation, she let slip the fact the I was down in Baja hunting. Well, the chief just darn near split a gut, and when I returned to my residency the following week, he came real close to firing me. Fortunately, my fellow residents came to my defense and calmed the old man down. Years later he

167

and I would laugh about it, but at the time I was seriously close to losing my job. This was my first trip back down since, and I was musing over those thoughts as I headed down the dusty schoolhouse road. Halfway to the pond, I came upon two boys in short sleeve shirts, no shoes, and with their thumbs out, trying to hitch a ride. There was already a chill in the air, so tonight would be *really* cold. I stopped and asked where they were going and they said to Trini's fish camp. That worked out well, because that was my destination also. They piled in, delighted to get a ride, and forty-five minutes later we were there.

Trini's served as a depository for American hunters' boats, trailers, dune buggies, and other hunting paraphernalia. For the adventurous there was even a landing strip, but it frequently flooded and was notoriously unreliable. I parked the van on the dike, pulled the boat off the car top, hooked up the motor, and got everything set for tomorrow. The two boys just stood around as if waiting for something. When I asked them why they didn't go home, they said they lived in Sombrerete and had come to Trini's to clean birds and fish. "Where do you stay at night?" I asked.

They had no plans, and just curiously stared at me with big innocent eyes. We built a fire next to the van, and I gave them drinks but no food. In truth, I had come down to Baja with a skillet, seasonings, and butter, plus my Beretta. I planned to shoot my dinner. Whatever politician said, "You can't have guns *and* butter," had never been down to Baja for a duck hunt. The boys disappeared for a while, then returned with some discarded Spoonbill carcasses which they had raided from Trini's duck refuse pile. They broke off the feet and legs, put them on the grate over the fire, and watched as the heat puffed up the Spoonie's feet into crisp potato puff-like treats; "Spoonie frito," the boys called them. They also grilled the gizzards, livers, and hearts. An hour later they went back for more carcasses and ate well past my bed time.

At midnight I got out of the van and didn't see the

boys; only when I heard some whispering under the van did I see them, huddled under the engine block, which was still giving off some heat. I opened the van door and said, *"Muchachos, ¡Adentro!"* Eagerly, they scampered into the van.

When I awoke next morning at four, the jug water inside the van had frozen solid. Those kids would have been ice blocks had they stayed outside. They helped me launch, on what turned out to be a glorious day for duck hunting. There weren't many hunters, and I ended up smack dab in the midst of the flight pattern. That evening I returned with a Mexican limit of fifty ducks. I looked for the kids to clean the birds, but they weren't there. They probably had found some gringo who needed ducks cleaned or whatever, and had a new place to spend the night. They also could have gone back home, but I doubted it.

Once everything was loaded I headed back toward Lupe's where I'd take the easy way out and ask Don Emilio to clean the ducks. Dinner would be some of Mamacita's delicious *frijoles* with fresh *tortillas*, plus my contribution, Tecate. Don Emilio took the ducks, then came back to sit and talk with me. Although uneducated, he was an interesting man, keenly observant, and with ideas on how to fix many of the *indios'* problems. But tonight was different; he had a favor to ask in a medical vein. There was a teenage boy up near Sombrerete with a total body cast and a bone infection. He knew the Mexican doctors were doing a good job, but he just wondered if I would mind taking a look and offering any other suggestions, if needed. It was a diplomatic way to avoid complaining about the local docs, yet at the same time registering his concern with me.

"It is no problem," I told him. I was heading up north tomorrow, anyway. When I got there, however, I was totally unprepared for what I saw. A young Mexican boy in his mid- teens had been placed in a total body cast, with certain areas of plaster cut out. Because of the cast's weight, he was secured to a round piece of wood, like a round table top, and whenever he needed to be moved, the round table top was placed on edge, and he was rolled to that destination. This allowed him to lie outdoors in the daytime and go inside at night. It was effective, but I didn't know if I would care to be moved from place to place in such a manner. The other notable item was the suppurative drainage from the right femur area, around which the cast had been cut away. The smell was unmistakably bacterial; no doubt about it, this kid had osteomyelitis, or infection in the bone, probably at the site of one of his fractures. A brief look at his meds showed the local doctors had the right idea. The medicine he probably needed, however, was one of the antibiotics for penicillin-resistant staph. He was being kept amazingly clean, considering he lived in a mud floor adobe house, and the ever- present Baja dust and dirt were everywhere. I planned to come down several weeks later, and would bring a month's supply of drugs at that time. As it turned out, this young man stayed in his cast for six more months, recovering satisfactorily from both the osteo and the multiple fractures. To live down in Baja and survive you just have to be tough, and this kid was.

Several weeks later, Curran and I returned for a mid-January shoot. This trip was more laid back than usual, which meant arriving in the afternoon, not the wee hours of the morning. It was more a scouting trip than anything else, as the water had gotten so high that all the old duck areas were now under water. To do well in these circumstances, you had to put in the effort and do lots of scouting. This you did during daylight hours, hence the leisurely trip down.

The fine powder dust hung in the air as we turned at Sombrerete. Curran drove slowly, allowing the dust to settle as we headed down schoolhouse road. Several miles and fifteen minutes later, the dust had mostly settled, making the trip ever so much more pleasant. In the rear view mirror Mike spotted some yahoo bearing down on us going hell-bent-for-leather, with the intention of passing and making us eat his dust.

"Hang on," shouted Curran.

He goosed the Chili Relleño, and off we went, now just several car lengths ahead of the speeding truck. We raced like that for a mile or so when Curran asked, "Is the right side of the road still flooded up there a mile before the next canal crossing?"

"Was two weeks ago Mike, and it looked like it'd be a while 'til it dried out." The spot he had in mind was almost half a mile in length, just on the right half of the two lane dirt road, and had been flooded at least a month now.

"Brace yourself, I'm gonna pull into the left lane." This required negotiating a center divider of giant mud clods, but Curran pulled it off without a hitch. When we hit the left lane we were doing sixty, which was plenty unsafe.

Mike kept it at sixty, then eased off a bit, as a group of smiling, cheering, young Mexicans passed us and gave us the razzmatazz. Curran did his part perfectly, for the instant they pulled out of our dust cloud and bit for the right hand pass, they hit the water and brake lights at the same instant. Their truck continued apace with ours, the only difference being they had full brakes on and were sliding and fishtailing through the mud. As they slowed down, so did we, until they came to a stop. They were stuck in mud halfway up their doors, necessitating an exit via the windows. The driver shot us the finger and shouted *"Cabrones,"* but one of 'em gave us a grudging smile. They had been *had*.

"Want to winch 'em out, Mike?"

"Nah," he laughed, "This was an objectivity lesson. These boys need to think about that the next few days while they're digging their car out."

Two days later when we headed back home, they were still there, digging.

We stopped in at Lupe's, and were met with a thunderous roar from the TV set we had given them for Christmas. Lupe had pestered us about it for three months, so finally we had purchased a black and white twelve inch set at the local second hand shop. It was run off a car battery which was convenient, because usually Lupe's '60 Impala wasn't running. We could already see what a mistake we had made, however, as this TV was like all others in Baja; it was turned up to maximum volume loud enough to be essentially unintelligible, and had the ugly effect of disturbing the serenity of this otherwise peaceful place.

It was a somber mood, indeed, with which the family greeted us. Before I could ask, "*¿Qué es la problema?*", Mamacita, half-sobbing, told us that "*Lupe está en la cárcel.*"

Whoa. That was not the kind of news we wanted to hear.

"*¿Qué pasó?*" I asked.

The gist of the explanation was that two *gringos* had walked up to Lupe in Coahuila and asked him to carry some marihuana across the border for them. The money was good, thirty bucks, but as he was to find out, it was poor pay for four years he was to spend in jail ... a Mexican jail. Over the next four years, the family would sell all two hundred of their goats, all the pigs, and turn every cent of their hard earned pesos into an effort to free Lupe from prison. Exactly how they did this, I am unsure, but my impression was it wasn't through the court system. Basically, Lupe just languished in jail until the authorities wanted to get rid of him. I will say this; he was a chastened man when he finally got out. Say what you want to about Mexican prisons versus American ones, but when Lupe was finally freed, he had no desire to do anything illegal *ever* again. Whatever the Mexican system of redemption was, it certainly made an impression on Lupe. Once out, he was no longer the wheeler-dealer, "bug-you-'til-you-give-him-something," that he once was. Lupe came out of prison a straight-arrow, and has remained that way since. Once, years later, when Curran asked him what it was like in a Mexican prison, he clammed up and walked off. Whatever it was, it must have been bad.

For Curran, this was his last trip for the year, but I still had one planned in February with two other hunting buddies, Dan and Paul. Paul's trips always took me three or four months to get over, so it would be good to go down with him at the *end* of the season.

No sooner was I home than Dan and Palmer called, to make sure the trip was still on in three weeks, and also to find out how the hunt had been with Mike. I told them about Duarte's high water and Lupe, both of which were discouraging, but Paul brightened my day with the news that he had finally figured out where those geese went when they flew southwest out of Duarte pond.

It was this thought of finally catching these geese in their hideaway that raced through my mind as we headed south towards the burned out railhead, el Doctor, down the straight asphalt highway that neatly splits the desert in half. At seventy miles per hour, everything looked the same in the dark, but Paul knew exactly where to turn off. We stopped for a moment to put his Suburban in four-wheel drive, then headed due west into the sand and dunes. There were no car tracks to indicate Paul had been here before, but he drove with the assuredness of a man who knew exactly where he was going. Suddenly, as if on cue, we pulled up to a mesquite-fenced corral, and saw the goats within. "We're here," announced Paul. A quick check on my watch said it was three a.m.

"Jeez, Palmer. All this way to hunt goats in a pen." It was Dan.

"Take it easy, this is just where we take off from. With luck we'll be there right at first light."

Right at first light meant five forty-five. We had a two hour and forty-five minute trek ahead of us and all I could see past the goat pen was thick, impenetrable mesquite trees. We had already decided each man would take two sacks of decoys plus gun and ammunition. It was Paul's hunt, so of course, there was no food or water.

As Paul had said before, "If I can take ten more shells instead of a sandwich, then that just improves my chances on the hunt." Always looking on the upside, he never allowed for any mishaps, hunger, thirst, or what-have-you. Some folks get up in the morning and think, "What a beautiful day." Paul would get up and think, "What a beautiful day for hunting." It sounds crazy, but around people like that, you yourself start thinking, "Hey, I don't need this Gatorade; this march is gonna be a cinch."

Fifteen minutes later, I proved that thought wrong. The mesquite grabbed the decoy bags, the clothing, and the guns; the mud sucked up our feet, legs and knees, making each step seem like slow motion. Although all three of us were in good physical shape, by three-thirty we had our tongues hanging out.

"How much more of this, Paul?" I asked. "My tongue's dragging in the mud."

"We'll take a blow here for five minutes, I'll get my bearings, and we'll head out again."

"Get his bearings? Who was he kidding?" I wondered. The mesquite was so thick that you couldn't see the stars, and with no moon, direction was based strictly on intuition, nothing else. Paul claimed he could see a star to the west, and every now and again he got a fix on it. Naturally, he had no compass.

Four more breaks later, I was well past beginning to feel my age. We had slowed to merely a snail's pace, but Paul was as expectant as ever. "Another fifteen minutes and we should be there."

It was overcast, so when first light came, everything just kind of turned grey. There was no real direction from which the dawn came. We were in mesquite and pea soup, and all points of the compass looked the same. I noted that my two compatriots had pulled a fast one and each had ditched one of their bags of decoys. If they thought we were going to find them again when we walked out of here, they were badly mistaken. Wherever we took a step, the mud, water, and mesquite closed over as if no one had ever been there. It was spooky, but not half as spooky as watching the sun come up in our faces ... from the west.

"Palmer, unless the world has just ended, that's the sun coming up, and we are walking due east, not west, you *putz*."

"That can't be right. I've had a fix on that star the whole time; it . . ."

Before he could finish, we suddenly broke out of the mesquite into a clearing, next to a goat pen, and . . . our Suburban. Palmer had managed to lead us through three hours of torture, to end up exactly where we had started. We had walked in an entire circle, yet not one of us, experienced hunters all, had the slightest indication we were making a perfect circle.

"Paul, you dumbshit." It was the only thing Dan had said since we left.

I didn't mention how much easier it was to pack the decoy bags back in the Suburban, since we now had two less bags than when we began. Paul was already going through the mental gymnastics of where we could go now; I could see in his eyes that he was going through all possible combinations and permutations, trying to figure what we could do with the rest of this hacked up day. The closest place was Huelton Canal, then back on up near the sloughs behind Luis B. Encinas. This late in the morning it would be our only shot, though we remembered full well burying the Suburban in suck mud several trips back.

A more direct route took us near the mud bogs and vehicle traps, but Paul felt lucky and maneuvered safely through them. As we got close enough to Luis Encinas to see the water tower, the Suburban sank in what appeared to be completely dry ground. The front tires went over it, but the back tires broke through, and the Suburban was mired in the muck . . . again.

By now Dan was used to Palmer's shenanigans, and when he got out, he already had the shovel in hand. It looked like this was going to be easy, but after forty five minutes of digging, Dan just succeeded in allowing the rear end to sink deeper.

"We're going to have to jack it up, Paul. Give me your jack."

"What jack? I didn't bring it."

"You what? Paul, you are a piece of work. You really didn't bring a jack on this trip? I mean, what if we had a flat or something?"

Paul just shrugged. Why he didn't bring it, God only knows. The fact was we had *no* jack. There was no hunting nearby, as the swamps were three or four miles from us. The only solution now was to walk into Luis Encinas, borrow a jack, and come back here.

As it turned out, we were farther from Luis Encinas than I had guessed; the hike into town took a little over two hours. Once there, we discovered that there were no autos in town, so we would have to walk into Coahuila, and that was ten to fifteen more miles. Luis Encinas is nothing more than some adobe huts with a beer parlor; there are no shops. Coahuila it was going to be.

We had walked several hours through the backroads when finally an old beat-up truck came by, loaded with *campesinos*. There is always room for one more, but three more severely tested the capacity of the truck. Dan ended up standing on the running board and hanging on to the side mirror. As it turned out, this was the only truck that would use this road for the next several hours, so we were lucky. Once in Coahuila, we started at the *ferretería*, or hardware store, but no jack. Next, we tried the automotive supply houses, and again, no luck. The tire shops were a thought, but they all had in-ground hydraulics. "I don't believe this Stanton, what's the word for 'jack' in Spanish?"

"I don't know, Paul."

"Well, how do you know they don't have 'em then?"

"First, I asked if they had a 'jack' and nobody understood English, so then I said, *"La cosa para levantar un auto "*– the thing with which to raise a car.

"Let's go back to the hardware store and try again."

"Okay Paul, but they don't have it. Even if I don't know the word, I can describe it well enough so they know what I'm talking about. Remember, I lectured in both Spain and Argentina in Spanish. Those folks knew what I wanted."

Once back in the hardware store, I tried again. In Spanish I asked for a 'jack;' "A thing with which to raise the car, a tool to raise the car up so we can get out of the mud;" and on and on. After fifteen minutes of this, Paul finally accepted that they didn't have what we were looking for. Resignedly, we made for the door. Just as we stepped out, an authoritative voice behind us asked, "*Señores*. How can I help you?" It was the owner, and he listened while I once again tried to explain what we wanted in Spanish.

Finally, the light went on, and he smiled as he said in English, "Ah, *señores*, you want a '*jacke*'." Smiles broke out all around; the *gringos* wanted a *jacke*. Why didn't they just ask for it in the first place?

We got our jack, and Palmer sweet-talked some *patrón* with a shiny new truck to drive us back to our vehicle. Once he dropped us off, we had the Suburban jacked up and out of the mud in no time. By now it was too late to hunt, and disgusted at losing the whole day, Dan looked at me and said, "Why didn't you just ask for the damn *jacke* to start with?"

I would have explained, but it probably wouldn't have done much good. On the way back to camp, I started thinking about the *jacke* and had a really good chuckle. It was just one more little incident, but I smiled as I realized how much I truly loved it down here.

Glossary

adentro – inside
a donde van? – where are you going?
afuera – out
ajojoli – sesame
aquí – here
arroyos – desert wash: dry river bed

bandidos – bandits
bucón – bass
buen tiro – good shot: also good shoot
buena salud – good health
buena suerte – good luck
buenas noches – good evening
buenos días – good morning

cabrón – "F"er
cabrones – male goats
cafe dulce – sweet coffee
cállete! – shut up
campesinos – country folk
capitán – captain
cartuchos – cartridges
cascabel – rattlesnake
casitas – little houses
cerveza – beer

chili colorado – spicy red stew
chinga – "F"-word
chingado – "F"ed
chiste – joke
chubasco – storm (as in hurricane) over the Sea of Cortez
churo – young goat
commandante – commander
con estos – with these

dinero – money
difícil – difficult

ejido – little village
el Día de gracias – for Mexicans Sunday: also day of giving
                  thanks (American Thanksgiving)
electricidad – electricity
el general – general
en el agua – in the water
entradas – entries
es bueno – is good
es imposible – is impossible
esta – is
estación – station
esta embarazada – is pregnant
es un médico? – are you a doctor?

Federales – Mexican federal troops
ferretería – hardware store
frijoles – beans

gracias – thank you
grande – big
gran fiesta – big party
gringos – Caucasians

hectares – 2 1/2 acres
huevos rancheros – eggs with Mexican salsa and chilies

indios – indians

jalapeños – hot peppers

kilómetro – kilometer

la cárcel – jail
la cosa – the thing
la frontera – the border
la grulla – sandhill crane
la vida – life is very hard
lisa – mullet
lonche – Tex-Mex for "lunch"

mano a mano – hand to hand
medicinas – medicines
menos de – less than
me permite? – may I?
mi familia – my family
mire – look
mordida – literally "bite" but is slang for bribe
muchachos – boys
mucho suerte – much luck

negocio – business
no te preocupas – don't worry

panadería – bread store
para levantar – to raise
patos – ducks
patrón – owner
pequeño – small
perro – dog
policía – police
por la Rumorosa – through Rumorosa
por que? – why?
pueden a limpiarlos? – are you able to clean them?

puro nada – "pure nothing" as in absolutely nothing

que es? – what is?
que fiesta – what a party
que paso? – what happened?
quien – who

salsa verde – green chili sauce
saludo a mi amigo – salute to my friend
Sedue – Mexican department of Fish and Game
señor – mister, sir
sí – yes
sientese – sit here
supermercado – supermarket

Tecate – wonderful Mexican beer brewed in Tecate
tenemos una problema – we have a problem
tenemos unas cosas para ustedes – we have a few things
for you
todos – all

una problema – a problem
un inyección – one injection

vamos a platicar – let's talk
ven aquí – come here
verduras – vegetables
viene – come